Much Afraid Little One

Unwanted, Abandoned, but Not Forsaken

"When my father and my mother forsake me,
then the Lord will take me up."
Psalm 27:10

Abbye Sue Binger

xulon
PRESS

Much Afraid Little One
Unwanted, Abandoned, but Not Forsaken
by Abbye Sue Binger

Printed in the United States of America.
Editing by Xulon Press

ISBN 9781498449946

www.xulonpress.com

TABLE OF CONTENTS

ACKNOWLEDGEMENTS

This book was an idea brought to me by a few close friends and family members. First, I wish to thank my dear friend, Marie for giving me ideas for the title of the book. Thanks need to go to couple of friends of my husband who encouraged me to write this book. I also would like to thank my beautiful daughter, who is a writer herself, for her suggestions in the process of writing the book. However, the most thanks need to go to Sarah, my special friend, who has spent countless hours helping me create word pictures for this story and editing the manuscript. Sarah worked painstakingly with me, transcribing and editing the manuscript over a period of more than three years. I can't thank her enough for her labor of love! Lastly, I want to thank my husband, who also contributed his time and effort to this project.

DEDICATION

This book is dedicated to my loving and devoted husband, our five children (including one in Heaven), along with our many friends who have brought the meaning of true friendship and acceptance into our lives. It is with their encouragement, support, and love that this story is being told. May it give a voice to those children who have no voice, and help those who greatly need someone in their corner.

INTRODUCTION

Amie and I met at a very early age, and it seemed throughout life, her life intermingled with mine. I've always seen myself as being nudged along, as if there was a good shepherd moving me in a certain direction. I believe Amie has the same good shepherd, and it is with this motive that I want to share her story.

When writing a book, no one has any inkling of what will be printed or how long it will take to finish. It always begins with an idea or a recurring thought. Amie and I began the process of writing this book almost seven years ago with the encouragement of friends who thought this particular story had to be told. It was time to let the "cat out of the bag," expose dark secrets in the light of healing, and be free of unseen chains. Once these chains were able to be broken, it brought forth the long desired wish for true freedom. This provided a greater opportunity to explore new territories that were once forbidden, creating an environment to learn about the many options in life that were not available before.

The premise of this book is to tell a meaningful, truthful, teachable, thought-provoking, emotional, hopeful, and sometimes funny story about a little girl named Amie and her struggles to make it in the world.

This narrative could have been anyone's story in her circumstances. As this story unfolds, the reader will get an inside look at what she was up against, and how these incidents affected her life. Amie's perceptions were determined by how she interpreted and internalized these incidents. A number of people who were involved in her life might not have seen these incidents in the same way. For their sakes, as well as for Amie, their names have been changed for the purpose of writing this narrative. The goal in telling this story is to help Amie come to terms about what happened in her past. It's about being an overcomer, as she worked through a very emotional process which included forgiving those who harmed her, whether they knew it or not. This process gave her the courage and strength to accept herself and not be ashamed anymore. She learned that real love and acceptance are the true underlying forces that give one the power to move forward which can only come through faith.

Amie's desire in telling her story is to offer hope to others who may be feeling stuck in similar past experiences. She discovered the ability to look at her life realistically and face the truth through a very angry, heart wrenching, and courageous process. Her secret to obtaining success was finding out what was true and throwing away the lies that were taught as if they were true.

It took working through these experiences which taught her that she could gain a true sense of value. Amie learned how to find help from trusted friends who believed in her, professionals, and people she met along the way whose encouragement gave her the inner strength to keep going. John 8:32 reads, "...And you shall know the truth, and the truth shall make you free."

BACKGROUND INFORMATION

When reading our favorite fairytales, we imagine everything working out in a magical and dreamy way with the characters living happily ever after. Like our much loved fairytales, Amie's life began in a very dark and lonely place. She was a child born out of wedlock to a young teenage girl who was involved with a man on heroin. Amie was the first of three girls who were also raised without a father. At the time of Amie's birth, there were very few options available for her teenage mother to care for her baby on her own. The news of her pregnancy put her family into shock, so much so that her father suffered a heart attack. Her mother was devastated and didn't know what to do. As a family they decided that when little Amie was born, she would have to be put up for adoption. Amie's mother was encouraged to "do the right thing" for this baby and place her with a family that could provide a "better" home. At least this way her baby would have a chance to be somebody someday.

For the most part, society at that time was very different in its view of what made up a family and how the family was expected to behave. Most people believed in a traditional marriage. The definition of a family was thought of as a mother, a father, their children, and the extended family. Any other kind of family would have been considered out of the norm, and

frowned upon. This attitude was reinforced to keep the status quo. Amie's mother and many other young teenage girls who had babies outside of marriage faced the same painful decision.

The process for Amie to be adopted did not happen right away. Her mother delivered her in a hospital near a home for unwed mothers in the early 1950's. She was born three months pre-mature, and weighed a little over two pounds. The likelihood of Amie's survival was doubtful due to her underdeveloped lungs and inability to breathe on her own. The treatments during these years were experimental as to how much oxygen would be needed to maintain life support for the health of an infant. There was an expectation that if Amie were to survive, she would have some level of neurological and visual issues due to the lack of oxygen to her brain. The real question was to what extent these issues caused damage.

From the moment of delivery, Amie's mother was not allowed to see her anymore. With regret and terrible sadness, she forfeited all parental rights. The state now became responsible for Amie's care. She remained in the hospital for almost two years due to her inability to thrive. Amie was alone, with no one to hold her, play or interact with her. She was in a dark and lonely place. A child remaining in a hospital for this length of time is called a "boarder baby."

The doctors used the time that she was in the hospital to monitor her and figure out where to place her. Her life was in their hands. One of the options being considered was placing Amie in an institution for those known as the "mentally retarded." This could have been a life sentence. It was thought of as taboo to keep a mentally or physically challenged child at home with his parents. To make it easier on the family and their community, it was viewed as a better option to put such a child "out of sight and out of mind." Without the support

systems that are in place today, the only option available was institutional care.

After Amie's second birthday, it was decided she could be placed in a temporary residence called a foster home. Foster care was designed to be a stop-gap measure for the protection of children from families in crisis. The objective was to give the child a "safe haven" until the crisis was resolved and the child could be reunited with his family. This process could last anywhere from a few months to a few years, because there were no limits in place on the family to resolve their crisis. If nothing worked out for the birth mother, then the only option left was adoption. The ultimate goal was to promote what was in the best interests of the child.

An Insider's Perspective of the Foster Care System

Before I share Amie's life story, I want to give insight into what it meant for her to be in the foster care system, and what it was like to be a foster child.

As most professionals in the field of early childhood development acknowledge, the early years of a child's life are considered the most formative years. What the child has been exposed to in these years will determine how a child learns to survive and build connections with other people. Amie didn't have the opportunity to feel that she belonged to anyone. She was just there with other foster children, hoping that someone would take her into her heart. If this longing could be fulfilled, there would be a real possibility for her and the other foster children to grow properly.

All children need to be wanted and cherished. In order to thrive, an environment needs to be created for the child to experience life intellectually, psychologically, emotionally and socially. These tools are a life-giving force for a child to establish her individual identity and belief system, which is an essential component in discovering where she fits in the world.

There is a poem written by Dorothy Law Nolte which speaks about these very things. It is entitled, "Children Learn What They Live," in which she writes:

If a child lives with criticism, she learns to condemn.
If a child lives with hostility, she learns to fight.
If a child lives with ridicule, she learns to be shy.
If a child lives with shame, she learns to feel guilty.
If a child lives with tolerance, she learns to be patient.
If a child lives with encouragement, she learns confidence.
If a child lives with praise, she learns to appreciate.
If a child lives with fairness, she learns justice.
If a child lives with security, she learns to have faith.
If a child lives with approval, she learns to like herself.
If a child lives with acceptance, and friendship, she learns to find love in the world.
(Copyright©1972/Dorothy Law Nolte)

The positive attributes in this poem reinforce the ideal of what every child needs to have in order to mature properly. The negative attributes in this poem make that process more of a challenge to overcome.

FOSTER CARE HOMES: THE EARLY YEARS

Amie's foster care years can be described as tentative, unclear, and definitely uncertain. The Jewish Child Care Association became responsible for Amie's custody and foster care placement. Her first placement into a foster home was very temporary. The foster family was told by the agency in charge of Amie's care that she was simultaneously being placed on a list for children designated for Willowbrook State School, located in Staten Island, New York, which was an institution for the severely handicapped and mentally retarded. Historically, Willowbrook was a state institution built in the late 1930's. Following World War II, it was used as an army hospital for disabled war veterans. During the 1950's and 1960's, Willowbrook housed handicapped children, and had a reputation for unethical medical practices. In 1965, Senator Robert Kennedy called this place "a snake pit." The living conditions were deplorable, leaving children to sit in their own feces. They were left alone, with no one to teach or care for them. Statistically, Amie would have been left behind with no real future, should that decision have been made. Therefore, Amie's stay in the foster home was on standby, her life was at risk and weighed in the balance.

For a two year old, Amie was severely behind in her development. All she could do was sit up and stare into space. She could not communicate her needs with facial expressions, or respond to others with words. Her only form of expression was through tears.

There was little to no success in Amie's progress with the first foster family. Therefore, the agency decided to give Amie more time with a new foster family to see if any progress could be made. This foster family was also told that Amie was being considered for Willowbrook. It turned out that this particular foster mother Flora along with her husband Jack had a real gift for taking care of children who were at risk. The decision to commit Amie to Willowbrook was put on hold once more with a "wait and see" approach. If Flora was successful on any level, then Amie would have a real chance for a future.

It would take two more years of psychological and physical testing to see if Willowbrook was inevitable. With each visit to the agency for physical and psychological testing, Amie improved and her doctors saw progress due to the intervention of the second foster mother. By the time she was four years old, she was able to talk, be potty trained, and walk with assistance of physical therapy and the use of two walking canes. Reaching for these canes was Amie's first real memory. During this time of enormous growth, Amie was finally diagnosed with Cerebral Palsy. This is an umbrella term used for brain damage that usually occurs during the birth process. She was no longer considered to be mentally retarded.

This turn of events was a real miracle for Amie. Flora took it upon herself to care for Amie. She felt that Amie "exhibited a soul," and believed that if she was given more time, she definitely had a chance to improve. Flora had previously cared for another child who was sent to Willowbrook and she did not want this to happen to Amie. She, in essence, saved Amie from

a potentially life-threatening existence in Willowbrook with no possibility for self-determination.

It must have been difficult for Flora to handle taking care of a disabled child while caring for up to two more foster children and three of her own at one time. She worked alongside the doctors and therapists, helping Amie to continue to progress and to function on par with other children her own age. What an accomplishment!

Flora and her family were a very traditional Italian Catholic family of the early 1960's, very different from Amie's biological family who came from a traditional Jewish background. As a result, Amie was exposed to two separate cultures, not really understanding to which she belonged. Flora was a good wife and mother-a stay at home mom who made sure everything ran smoothly. She did most of the housework, like laundry, ironing, cleaning and cooking. Her family pitched in with the cleaning of the house on Saturdays. Amie was not allowed to help, for fear that she would break something. Flora was a very good cook. Amie told me that she watched her cook most of the meals and developed what she called "Italian taste buds." Jack worked long hours as an airplane mechanic during the night shift. He was handy around the home and took care of mowing the lawn and painting. He liked to barbeque and help his wife with anything she asked of him. Amie was the oldest of three (sometimes four) foster children living in the home. They all shared one bedroom. The other foster children were much younger than Amie.

As Amie related her story to me, she found it difficult to put into words what it felt like to be a foster child. Emotionally, Amie — along with the other foster children — saw themselves unequal to the biological children in the home. When Amie started kindergarten, she realized that she was different from other children. At school she was treated like any other child that was part of the class. When she was home, she felt like an

outsider. There was a great gap between the household rules for the biological children verses the foster children. There were no freedoms to eat liberally, there were no second helpings and no snacking in between meals. Bathing was restricted to once a week. Toys, which were provided by the foster care agency, were used as a punishment tool and frequently disappeared and the children told the toys did not belong to them anyway. The foster children had little to play with and were never allowed to have playmates in the house.

Amie wore hand-me-downs and was dressed in boys' clothing when she was not at school, going to the town's local barber shop for haircuts. All the little girls at school had matching ribbons and barrettes in their hair, unlike Amie who had no one to fuss over her. She knew that her world was not the same as her peers'. In order to understand her perspective, you need to think of it as if you were watching other people play a sport, and you were not allowed to participate. There were no social activities that she was allowed to be part of where she could learn how life was supposed to be. Bedtime was always promptly at six o'clock in the evening. "There was no tucking in or saying good night, just the sound of the eye and hook lock on the outside of the door to keep us in," Amie told me. She said her life could be summed up as if she were simply a chicken in a hen house. Amie was left feeling like no one liked her, and it reinforced her deep sense of loneliness, of not belonging to anyone, and feeling very unloved.

Amie was not aware that her birth mother was still in the picture and had the legal right to keep her. Amie's mother was going for drug rehabilitation in hopes of getting her little girl back. She was not allowed any kind of physical contact with her during this process. Her attempts were unsuccessful, and seven years later Amie's biological mother regretfully gave up and signed the adoption papers.

A POSSIBLE ADOPTION

An adoptive home was finally found for Amie. There was a Jewish couple with two boys who wanted a little girl to complete their family. Amie, now seven years old, was a little nervous and wondered to herself why this family would want her. After all, the foster family was all she knew. Amie pondered whether or not this they would like her and keep her. She did not know what to expect because this family was not Italian like the foster home.

The day finally arrived! It was time to leave the foster home and move in with her adoptive family. Her new parents were very kind and warm, and welcomed her with open arms. They really liked her. This gave Amie a feeling of hope that this family would work out after all. Her new mother dressed her up to look feminine. Amie had a "little miss" wardrobe with skirts, pretty tops and dresses, tights and patent leather shoes. Amie suddenly looked like a little girl and felt like one too! With her new family came a new school, a Hebrew Day School. This school was very different from the one she knew. The morning schedule was devoted to traditional classes of reading, writing, arithmetic, science, and social studies. The afternoon program focused on learning Hebrew and Jewish Culture. All the girls in her school wore a jumper, a white blouse, tights, and black shoes. The boys wore dark pants, with a white shirt and black

shoes. Amie recalled finally feeling she was part of the group. She did not feel unwanted anymore.

Yet, Amie knew life was full of mixed emotions and there were so many changes to which she had to adjust. Everything was different, from the clothing, the food, the cultural traditions and beliefs to learning how to live with boys. She was no longer in a Catholic home but was put into the midst of a very traditional Jewish home, with very little understanding of what that meant. She missed Italian food, Christmas, and Easter. She found it very hard to understand the new religious holidays she was expected to observe. Amie was happy to be wanted, yet felt "bad" at the same time. She was taught by the foster family that being Jewish was not a good thing. Their children often teased Amie, saying, "The Jews killed Christ." The foster parents never objected to this statement from their children, at least not in front of Amie. She tells me, "I felt sad for Jesus, and didn't want to say anything to hurt my new family." Amie kept this a secret in her heart for many years. She was torn between two worlds. For a "much afraid little one," this was too scary for her to embrace. She did not want to be a bad girl.

While at school, Amie remembers trying to copy the Hebrew letters off the blackboard onto special note paper. She really did not understand the lessons and did not learn much. Amie was also experiencing growing pains in her hips and in the back of her knees. This was agonizing and made her cry a lot, making it difficult to concentrate on her studies. Her new parents took Amie to the doctor to find out what caused these pains, and were told that it was normal for her age. She remembers not understanding what was happening to her body. There was no real explanation given to Amie, and this compounded the confusion she felt about herself.

Being a seven year old girl with a curious nature, Amie found herself exploring her new mother's dresser, something she could

never do at the foster home. She was fascinated with her pretty, glittering, and shiny perfume bottles. As Amie was touching and trying one of the bottles, it spilled all over the dresser! Amie expected to get severely punished for this and tried her best to clean it up. When her new mother found out what she had done, her first reaction was shock, and then disappointment. Amie did not remember any significant punishment, other than feeling terrible. Soon after this a social worker showed up, at the Jewish family's request, asking Amie if she would like to go back to her old foster home. What a question!

The idea of being placed back in the foster home must have come from Flora herself. She was the only one who could have made this possible. Amie really thought the foster family did not want her around anymore. She knew at the bottom of her heart that Flora really must have cared for her, even though she never told her outright. Her mannerisms where always approachable and trustworthy. Amie told me, "I felt safe in her presence because she was the defender of the foster children." She was their champion. Amie became so excited about the prospect of going back to her home. She had hopes that the family had missed her and wanted to adopt her. Maybe now she could be part of their family after all.

For the adoptive parents, it became obvious that Amie would need more physical and emotional care than they could provide.

By the end of the school year, being overwhelmed, the parents asked the agency to take her back. It was explained to Amie that they were not a good match. As Amie was leaving their home, the parents reassured her that even though she could not stay with them, they were going to put money away for her to go to college. This left Amie with the impression that she could have a future.

BACK THERE AGAIN

The time had come for Amie to go back there; to the family she so desperately wanted to join. Filled with excitement and wonder, she thought, "Is this really happening? Do they really want me?" Amie's heart was filled with new hope that it was going to work out this time. She did not notice or care if she had any of her new clothes or other "girly" things that the other family had given her. Her only focus was on becoming a real member of this Italian family. She wanted to be their daughter. All of Amie's hopes were set on being accepted. The questions continued in her childlike heart as she wondered if they would welcome her with open arms and if they had truly missed her.

As she arrived at her old foster home, Amie was finally back where she wanted to be — or so she thought. The days went by and she found that her surroundings and status in the foster home really did not change. She sat on a cot in the old, tiny room she shared with the other foster children, who came and went. As she did, Amie suddenly realized this was not her world. All of her hopes of being part of the family began to fade away. She craved their love and attention, anticipating they would want her and be proud of her, but this never came to pass. It was as if the hope Amie built up around herself was merely a glass dream that shattered all around her. She never received the

love she needed. Amie was left feeling so disappointed and felt so terribly alone, again.

The words would often echo in Amie's mind, "We took you back out of the kindness of our hearts. And don't you forget it!"

These words of the foster parents' children, spoken on a persistent basis, damaged Amie's already broken heart. Many times these kinds of things were said when Flora was out of the room. However, even though she didn't intend to, Flora closed her eyes to this behavior towards Amie. One of the children was especially aggressive and would slap the foster children at will if she did not like something they did. Also, she would often make Amie think that she was going to get into trouble. The one comfort Amie was left with was to lay on her cot at bedtime and hit her head against the pillow until the pain in her heart would stop. She would not have to agonize about what the next day would bring, as exhaustion would set in so that she could finally sleep.

There was a little foster child whose name was Jonathan who touched the hearts of the foster family. Jonathan was a very cute blonde-haired, blue-eyed boy. He liked to do boy things and followed the foster father everywhere, doing what he was doing. Jack really got a kick out of him, and enjoyed taking care of him. He liked the idea of having a son around, since his own children were all girls. Amie remembers hearing talk about the foster parents wanting to adopt him. When Jonathan's biological parents found out, they immediately had him returned to them. The foster parents took this very hard, and so did Amie, but for different reasons. "Why would they be willing to adopt Jonathan and not me?" Amie would ask herself. Amie felt doubly rejected. Her only wish to be adopted by them did not come true, because they chose someone else. It was something that just had to be accepted, no matter how much it hurt. Amie learned to keep quiet about it. All of her disappointments, anger, sadness and

frustration were stuffed deep down inside of her little soul. She knew better than to express any of her feelings because the foster family was bound to take it personally, and then there would be slapping or other punishments. Amie explained:

> "There was always an underlying threat of being put out of the home if any of us didn't tow the line. We knew better than to say anything or have a temper tantrum that would make the foster family look bad or embarrass them. We always had to keep up appearances to make them look good, even if at times it was a lie. We were left without a voice with no one to listen."

This kind of atmosphere in the home created a tremendous amount of fear, anxiety and worry for all the foster children. The foster family used intimidation as a vehicle to keep Amie and the other foster children under control, but in their view they were providing a "roof over their heads and food in their bellies." For them, it was a noble and decent thing to do.

Those in authority, such as the social workers, medical staff, and the psychological staff were not really aware of what happened during the ins and outs of the foster children's day-to-day lives. From time to time a social worker would come out to the foster parents' home to check up on how things were going. Amie would pretend everything was fine because she did not feel safe to say what she was really feeling. The social worker missed the subtle negative clues as to what was actually going on. The foster care agency and the foster parents' objective was to offer what they considered to be in "the best interest" of the children. In a natural family setting, ideally, both parents impart an atmosphere of love, nurturing, provision, protection and teaching. In the foster care setting, the parental role is divided up between

everyone involved with the foster child's life. The problem was, however, that Amie only received bits and pieces of this vital objective.

The only identity a foster child understands is seeing himself as a foster child. There was no feeling of belonging, having value, or experiencing pride as an individual. Amie says, "I missed out. I felt like I was just there, taking up space that didn't belong to me. We weren't cherished or nurtured." In the world of the foster child, the system labeled the children with no other identity, forcing them to look to the outside in hopes for a better, positive sense of self.

Keep in mind that for many biological children, it was natural for them to experience jealousy. This was due to the fact that their mother probably took more time away from them caring for the foster children. Yet the real reason for this was that the foster children were more needy since they did not have parents or a family of their own. Amie was a child with more physical needs than the other foster children.

> "What Flora's own children did not understand was that she was always going to be their mother, and that they would never have to experience losing her while they were still children. The hard thing for them to accept was that the foster children viewed her as their mother as long as they lived in their home."

During this time, Amie began to take on the responsibility of the other foster children that were there. She tried to make them understand that they had better behave so that they could stay there, and be "good" so that they would not get into trouble. She was not always successful at it.

THE FIRST OPERATION

When she was about seven years old, Amie's vision began to change. Her doctors noticed that her left eye began to turn inward towards her nose. In layman's terms, this is called being cross-eyed. The muscles in her eye were weak, and this caused it to look crossed. She was required to do various exercises to help her strengthen her eye muscles and return her eye to its place. One of the exercises Amie remembers was to color in a coloring book with a red filter on top of the page. Amie had to wear a patch over her strong eye, making it very tedious. She worked so hard with all of the exercises, but none of them worked well enough to repair her eye. The only option left was to have the eye surgically corrected.

Amie was very scared and frightened to have to go to the hospital for the operation. No one was there to help her understand what was about to happen and calm her anxieties. She did not even know what an operation was or the purpose of a hospital. Because she didn't know anyone who had gone to the hospital, she felt it had to be pretty bad.

> "The walls were white, and the nurses wore white uniforms with white hats having a black or blue stripe on them. There were no pictures on the walls. The bed was a big metal crib, and had high

bars on the sides so that she could not get out. It felt like a prison, and nothing in the hospital was warm or comforting."

Still, being a curious little girl, she asked why there was a stripe on the nurses' hats. One of the nurses replied that each color represented the nursing school from which they had graduated.

Amie does not remember being brought to the hospital, or many of the details after she arrived, yet one memory stands out. Just right before the operation, a nurse told her to breathe into a plastic cup filled with ether that was held over her nose. Amie went on to relate that,

> "The nurse said to me, 'This will put you to sleep so that you won't feel anything.' But, to everyone's surprise I woke up in the middle of the operation. I remember the bright lights, and the doctors and the nurses talking. One of nurses told me that everything was all right, and that I could go back to sleep. It was a little scary, but I didn't feel any pain."

The doctors called the surgery a success and put a patch over Amie's left eye so that it would heal. She saw double for a few days while her right eye did the work. During her week-long stay in the hospital, the nurses kept her company because she had no visitors. Amie day-dreamed about going to the foster family's summer home. There were other families with children who enjoyed playing with Amie and the other foster children. It was nice to have a change of pace.

Amie was told by her doctor that when she got home from the hospital she would need a pair of glasses. Flora took her to

an optometrist to pick them out. She chose pink speckled ones, and thought they were so pretty. What an exciting moment for Amie! This was the first time she was allowed to pick out anything for herself. Her new glasses helped her read the blackboard in school, as well as watch television. Her doctor said that the glasses were also to be used for the movies, but she never got the chance to go while she was still living with that foster family.

EARLY EDUCATIONAL EXPERIENCES

For Amie, being in school was very tough. She realized she looked different from her peers due to her disability. She felt ashamed that she was not like the other children, in part because she had to wear leg braces to help her walk during the day, as well as a bar brace worn between her legs at night. They were very ugly to look at. She wore army-type boots made of leather. Walking was always a challenge since there was a steel bar attached to the bottom of the boot, and a strap under and around her knees. They were very heavy. The leg braces helped keep her calf muscles stretched and kept Amie off her toes. She made the two block journey to school and back in her braces, every day, rain or shine. Still, this made it difficult for her to run around with the other children during recess time. Fortunately, none of them made fun of her, yet not many of her fellow students spent much time with her during lunch or free play. Amie would sit near a teacher and watch as the others played.

One of the best memories that always brings a smile to her face is her kindergarten graduation. She was all dressed up in a new dress with curls in her hair. She was allowed to take off the leg braces and wear pretty patent leather shoes. Amie was so surprised when one of the teachers picked her up off the stage

and put her on the floor. She was the first to receive her diploma and did not have to walk down the stairs for it.

At night she had to wear the bar brace. This too had army-type shoes, except it only had one steel bar connecting the shoes to keep her feet still. It was welded on by a big bolt on the back of each shoe. The purpose of this brace was to help keep her feet from turning inward. One foot was pointed to the far left, while the other was pointed to the far right. A good night's sleep was out of the question. Amie would be woken up every time she tried to turn on her side, and her knees would knock together and whack the shoes against the wall. Every time this happened, Amie experienced pain, and it happened again and again throughout the night. Since she was not able to turn over, she ended up sleeping on her back, making it more uncomfortable. Often, the shoes were tied too tight, causing pain to her ankles. To make things worse, since Amie and the other foster children were put to bed at six o'clock at night, she would often need to get up and use the toilet before too long. Amie, waddling to the bedroom door, braces and all, pleaded and knocked on the locked door to get out and go! Sometimes she did not make it without an accident. Amie would be too afraid to tell anyone, so she would go back to bed in soiled clothing, hoping that by morning the wet clothes would be dry and no one would be the wiser. Eventually, she learned it was easier to hold it until morning. After all this, the night brace did not accomplish its purpose. Amie does not remember wearing it after grade school.

When Amie moved on to the first grade, learning became more difficult. The cerebral palsy caused a learning disorder called visual perception disability, making it difficult for Amie to process what she saw. It was apparent to Amie that she saw things at slower pace than her peers, creating a need for more time to understand what was in front of her. However, once she was able to grasp what was being taught, it began to make sense

for her and she could move on with her work. She preferred to hear the instructions and lessons a couple of times. This gave her the confidence to remember them better.

Reading was the hardest of all her subjects. As she looked at a sentence, she saw nothing but a blur, instead of the letters and words she was expected to read. Amie taught herself to separate the letters and to form them into words a little at a time. This was so tedious, and she was so focused on finding out what the words were, that she forgot all about what they meant! Then there was the problem Amie had with copying what she saw written on the blackboard. For her to read, remember and then write on a piece of paper what she saw on the blackboard was an overwhelming task for her because of the way her brain worked. In the process, she lost a lot of the words simply because she just could not see them or keep up with the class, and the words were being erased before she could write them all down. Amie, a little pioneer, was using her own learning curve since special education was not understood as well as it is today.

Third grade was another hurdle she had to face. She ended up being held back because she did not understand or master the concept of subtraction in arithmetic. Amie had trouble lining up the numbers in the correct columns. She did not realize that addition was just the opposite of subtraction, and could not retain the answers in her head. She ended up using her little fingers to help her find the answers. No matter how hard Amie tried to count correctly, she was always off by one number. She would say to herself: "What happened to my little fingers? Do I have more than ten? Did I count too many of them?" She told me: "No one taught me any tricks to help me get the right answers. I felt so defeated, and really dreaded going to school. I felt stupid. This feeling stayed with me for a very long time."

Amie also related:

"I can still remember many of the songs we learned in grade school, those many years ago, because of my gentle music teacher Mrs. Monday. I can still picture her in my mind. She wore her hair like a flat top with little bangs and cats eye glasses with little heels. She loved to teach and took pride in her students. She always encouraged us to do our best. She made me feel that I could do anything. Because of her, my love for music hasn't changed."

Even though Amie was not able to read well, she was able to learn the songs her music teacher taught her by listening to them over and over again. She always enjoyed being able to participate in the school chorus during school hours. Every week Amie would sway her body to the music and brighten the room with her big, beautiful smile. This is the first time Amie realized that she could learn something, and it made her happy.

With a new school year starting, Amie was encouraged to play an instrument in the school band. This was a fourth grade milestone and each child was given a chance to participate. Everyone was allowed to pick out the instrument they wanted to play. Amie was so excited that she could be involved and learn more about music. The band teacher helped her pick the clarinet because it was light enough to carry home and to practice. Learning to read the notes was a challenge for her, but her passion for music spurred her on to get it right. "Well, most of time, anyway," she said. She really enjoyed practicing and playing in the band. After a while, the foster family grew tired with having to hear her practice at home. They did not want to spend the spare change of buying reeds for the mouthpiece, either, which were only the price of a piece of bubble gum. By the end of the school year she was no longer in the school band.

Once again, Amie was severely disappointed, because the one thing she felt she could do well had been taken away from her.

Even so, Amie told me:

> "Because of the music teacher's influence in my young life, I decided when I grew up that I wanted to be a teacher. That goes to show teachers do have a profound influence upon their students. I will always remember that she took notice of me. She made me feel that I had value and was somebody."

During spring vacation Amie was around nine years old she came down with the mumps. She knew was that she had painful swelling in her throat and glands, and it was never explained to her why this was going on. Aside from the periodic check-ins from Flora she was left alone in her little room with no one to comfort her. All she could do was cry, and did not know if she would ever recover. This scared her. "It seemed like forever," she recalls. Gradually, the symptoms left her and she was able to go back to school.

On other school vacations, she came down with the chicken pox, and scarlet fever. As when she had the mumps, the same thing happened-she was left alone. Amie wondered what was happening to her body, and worried how long it would take to get better.

Fifth grade was the year of "do-overs" and tears. Amie was required to copy the same assignments over and over again until she got it right all year long. Her teacher did not understand that Amie couldn't see her mistakes, and she was facing the same visual issues from first grade. It just became more compounded with the increased amount of school work. Her papers

would come back with bright red marks all over them, along with the words "DO OVER!" in big letters. She worked hard to correct her mistakes, but always ended up with new ones. After the fourth or fifth redo, her frustration brought her tears, and a desire to say, "Forget it, I'm done!" Coming home from school never provided much relief. Flora felt Amie needed to be punished for her bad grades and thought this would straighten her out. Since Amie loved to watch television, she took this away. "It really didn't matter, nor help, because nothing really changed," she told me.

Throughout the early educational experiences shared here, there is a little more to add. Amie really enjoyed gymnastics in gym class, and it was her favorite. She really felt like the other children because everyone wore the same gym uniform. "We all had spotters, and wore these cute little gym shoes. They reminded me of what ballerinas wear." She was not able to do much of the jumping or running, but she enjoyed doing the mat exercises. "I was able to do a head stand with help while pointing my toes as I lifted my legs in the air!" Amie went on to say:

> "I don't remember much of what happened in sixth grade, except for graduation. All of the other girls were dressed up in pretty dresses, and had their hair done with headbands and curls. Sitting in the bottom row in front of all the class, there I sat dressed in a plain, long, oversized shirt with a ruffle on the bottom, and an unmatched skirt. My shoes were ugly, clunky, black oxfords, and my socks were scrunched down around my ankles. Wearing my pixie cut and smile, nobody knew that I felt like I stuck out like a sore thumb. I wasn't taught that I had value in my appearance, but it sure felt embarrassing."

With a bit of sadness, Amie shared her graduation picture with me, as she remembered all that had happened.

The next year Amie was supposed to go begin junior high school, but that didn't happen right away...

SLEEP AWAY CAMP

After Amie turned eleven years old, the agency decided that it would be a good experience for her to go to sleep-away camp to "be like other children." Everyone attending came from various communities throughout the state, and just came to have some fun. Amie tells me, "No one knew that I was a foster child. I was like everyone else. There might have been other foster children there, but I wasn't aware of them." The camp was located in the country and was surrounded by lakes and mountains. The children attending the camp were divided by age and there were no more than ten children in each group. Amie says:

> "[The rules at camp] didn't feel like rules, unlike the rules in the foster home. We had to keep our cabin and our bunk area clean. Sometimes there were contests between cabins as to who did the best job. It made work fun. The food was good, and I could pick out anything that I wanted to eat! No one told me what I could and couldn't eat, and there were always snacks. What a difference from the foster home."

Each day was divided up into activities. Amie liked arts and crafts, where she learned how to make lanyards. The camp

offered instructional swim. Amie learned to float and do the frog stroke on her back. She was not able to really swim because her hips would not cooperate. "I was terrified of the water, but hey, I dog paddled!" she exclaimed. Amie kept herself at the shallow end of the lake to feel safe. She remembers:

> "Being at sleep away camp gave me the chance to be myself. The counselors liked me, as did some of the other campers. I even made a few friends. It was such a relief to be away from the foster family and not worry about anything. I really didn't want to go home and was looking forward to coming back the next summer."

A Second Series of Operations

Before leaving for camp the following summer, when Amie turned twelve, her doctors were considering operating on the calf muscles of both legs, one at a time. She walked on her toes and had trouble with falling down, and they hoped she would walk with more stability and this would prevent her from falling. These operations were called "heel cord releases."

After having a great time at sleep-away camp, Amie returned with more than her doctors bargained for. She was covered in mosquito bites! "I was scratching all the time, and it was so annoying! It was hard to resist not scratching," Amie says. The doctors had to wait to perform the operations until the scabs disappeared, which took about a month. She went into the hospital terribly anxious about what was supposed to happen. The only consolation that helped to calm her fears was the hope that she would be able to walk better. Amie had no idea how long she would have to stay in the hospital or what the recovery time would be, nor did she understand what she would have to experience after the surgery.

Her first surgery took place towards the end of August — the hottest part of the year. The operation was performed by the Chairman of the Department of Orthopedics of the hospital

where Amie began her long stay. As Amie woke from the anesthesia, she was in extreme pain. She was surprised to see a plaster cast extending from the top of her right thigh all the way down her leg to her foot, leaving a little opening exposing her toes for air and wiggle room. Amie was moved to the pediatric orthopedic ward for monitoring and recovery.

Amie was confined to her hospital bed most of the time because she had to share the extended stretcher wheelchair with the other children on her ward. She recalls:

> "Boy, I didn't have the patience for that! This was the only time I could get out of the bed and not be alone! It was really hard for me to cope with the physical and emotional pain of the surgery. The entire ward was very hot since there were no air conditioners. Ceiling fans were always on...to try to keep us cool, but I was sweating all the time. I felt isolated and unwanted. It would have been easier for me to cope if the nurses or doctors had explained the 'why' of things."

Flora and Jack rarely went to see her. Their excuse was that at that time there was a lot of civil unrest, which included riots in the streets in the city. Amie thinks that they were just afraid to go there and see her. "I remember crying a lot, and no one could calm me down. I considered myself to be a bad patient. I would notice that other families came to see their children, and I felt left out," she said sadly.

After a couple of weeks, it was time to do the second surgery. Knowing what to expect, Amie was calmer, but she really did not want to have to go through it again. What was she going to do with two casts on? At least up to this point she had one free leg to work with. This time, the surgery was performed by

a medical resident under supervision. Waking from anesthesia, she realized just how little she could move. "Having both casts on my legs, half of my body didn't exist, and I really needed that wheel chair!" Amie says.

Soon after her second surgery, the doctors realized that the left cast was too tight around her toes. To fix it, they cut an opening around her toes and added more plaster to give them room to move.

> "It seemed one leg's pain was slowly subsiding, while the other leg was hurting really bad. It made my brain confused. I was such a mess. School was about to start, but I was in no shape to participate. Teachers from the city schools came in to teach the children on our ward according to our grade level. They worked really hard to help us learn, but I just couldn't concentrate. After a month or so, my legs began to really itch inside the casts. I cried out, and asked: 'Why are they itching so much?' I was told this meant they were healing and that the casts would come off soon."

Amie experienced great trepidation and anticipation when the day finally arrived to take the casts off. Amie was wheeled into an empty room on a stretcher and the first thing she noticed was a hand-held electric saw. She described her experience vividly:

> "My eyes opened wide and I began to cry. The doctor told me that they were going to use this saw to take the casts off. When I heard the noise the saw made I screamed and cried out: 'Are you going to take off my legs, too?' The doctor tried to

calm me down by saying, 'We are not going to cut off your legs.' But I didn't believe them. The vibration of the saw felt so close to my legs and kept me crying until they were finally taken off. When I first saw my legs, I thought they'd shrunk. It was like I had zippers in the back of my legs where the stitches were. One leg looked smooth, while the other looked all lumpy. The stitches were uneven and rough to the touch, like chopped meat. They still look the same. But at least I could walk now."

It was time to start physical therapy. The physical therapist would come into Amie's room and move her knees by bending them up and down. Amie cried and cried, saying, "You're hurting me!" The therapist tried to explain to her that it was going to hurt because she had not used her legs in over two months, and that her legs would go into spasms. This would only cause pain and she would end up screaming.

One doctor in particular spoke kind words to Amie, saying, "It will be worth it when you are able to walk on your own." This helped and comforted her somewhat and she became more cooperative.

"It seemed like a long process because my legs were weak. First, I had to be able to put weight on my legs. I would swing my legs over the side of the bed and try to stand up. I couldn't do it at first. My legs felt wobbly. I needed help. The therapist gave me a pair of crutches. They scared me because I thought I would tip over trying to use them. I never had to use them before and it took me a while to get the hang of it. Within a couple of weeks I was using them, and the doctors

decided I was walking well enough to go home. I didn't think so. But, whatever."

Flora and Jack came to pick Amie up from the hospital. It had been a very long time since she had seen them, at least three weeks. Amie was excited to leave the hospital, and at the same time was very nervous about going home. She did not know what to expect. The doctors gave explicit instructions for Amie not to use the crutches at home. They wanted her to be as independent as possible.

She did not experience the warm feelings that you would expect a child to feel when being picked up from the hospital by their family. On the contrary, she dreaded it, knowing that she would not be receiving the attention she had at the hospital once she was back at the foster home.

These operations, however had a very positive outcome for Amie. They had been a real success. She was now able to walk heel to toe, and more flat footed with the help of the leg braces that extended to her knees. The idea was that the braces were there to keep the calf muscles stretched until the doctors decided she was stable enough to walk without them, which took about a year. "These were the same ugly braces I had worn before," Amie said.

FORCED TO SAY GOOD-BYE

As soon as Amie was back in the foster family home, the crutches were taken away so that she would not be dependent upon them. "I would have felt better if they were weaned away from me gradually," Amie said. "It would have given me more confidence to walk without them. I felt forced to fend for myself. I held on to anything and everything in sight, including the walls, the furniture and the doors of the house." One time she was told to go outside to get some air. She really did not want to go outside, and no one went with her. "All I could do was to hold on to the bushes outside their home. I was afraid that I would fall and that made me mad and scared at the same time. They would not let me back in the house for a long time," Amie remembers.

This taught her, at a very young age, that she had to rely on herself to meet her needs. Her trust in others faded away as she experienced disappointment after disappointment and broken promise after broken promise. Trust was becoming a rare commodity. She was being treated more like a human being outside the foster home than in it. The blinders were coming off. Amie told me she knew something was up, "The secret's out! There was a double standard. I didn't have the same human rights as the foster parents' own children." Amie did not dare share her discovery with anyone.

It was during this year of recovery that many things were about to change in Amie's life. She began to feel a need to protect the other foster children in the home. Amie tried to make sure they followed the rules, so that they would not get hit.

> "One time, Jack hit a foster boy so hard, the boy turned purple. Flora cried out, 'Stop it! Stop it!' He finally stopped his rage, but it left me terrified. I would often remind the other foster kids, 'If you don't behave, they are going to hit us, or kick us out.' There was always a threat of some kind hovering over us."

One story Amie shared with me was when Flora left her in charge of the other foster kids. They had to go out for something with their girls, and there was no one to watch them. She was outside in their driveway with them playing when she noticed a car on their block that did not belong there. She thought that maybe it was one of the foster kids' parents and got really nervous. "I made the other foster kids run back into the house, so one of them wouldn't be kidnapped. After the foster parents got home, I told them what I saw, but they didn't say anything, not even a thank you." Flora made sure that the agency social worker knew what happened.

Coming upon the pre-teen years, Amie was becoming more aware of just how different she was from her peers. Amie said, with tears in her eyes:

> "I felt self-conscious that I still had to wear leg braces, because of the physical disability, and I was a foster child. Everyone knew, and I also thought that people felt sorry for me and didn't know how to be my friends. I was isolated most

of the time because of it. I really began to not to like myself because I thought I wasn't liked. I was so embarrassed. The idea of going back to school made me nervous. I was getting ready for seventh grade in a junior high school."

The school she would be going to was a combined junior and senior high school. "I ended up getting tutors because I wasn't ready to walk completely on my own. I hadn't been in school for over three months and had a lot of catching up to do." The school district assigned two tutors. One tutor focused on English and Social Studies, while the other tutor focused on Math and Science.

"The tutors were really kind and didn't get upset with me when I didn't get it. They gave me a lot of attention and encouragement. I don't know how much I learned, but they didn't make me feel like I was stupid. When I was in regular school, I was always frustrated about something. The work load went at a much faster pace, and I was always behind. They gave me a new sense of value."

Flora made the teachers very comfortable in her home. They taught Amie upstairs in the dining room. "It felt strange to me because staying upstairs was a forbidden area. Most of our daily activities were done in the finished basement. My tutors, of course, didn't know that. The dining room was reserved just for company," Amie recalled. The tutors took turns coming to the house for over two months, but this would be the last time that Amie would spend in their dining room.

"Stepping up on to the school bus for the first time in my life, I remember wearing a striped

dress, fishnet stockings, and my leg braces. Boy, that was a big step. By the time I got on, the bus started moving, so I grabbed my seat in the front really fast so that I wouldn't go tumbling down. Everything was new for me. One of the first things I had to learn was to memorize my locker combination so that I could put my coat and books away in between classes. I had more than one teacher now; a teacher for each subject. One teacher made me a little nervous because he was a man. I was shocked! All of my teachers in elementary school were women. There were so many things to adjust to, like bigger classrooms, kids I didn't know, lots of homework, girls were wearing make-up, etc. Also, I had a hard time walking to classes, and was always late getting there. The others were having fun, but it was hard work for me! Boys and girls were dating, and going to after school clubs, but not me. I felt like an odd ball. But one of the bright spots was that I ended up with three good friends."

Amie struggled really hard and needed the help of her teachers to complete the work load.

"I felt that I always came up short of the goal. It seemed to me that my classmates didn't have to struggle so hard to get A's and B's. I only managed to stay just above passing with grades in the low seventies. Even so, the teachers encouraged me to keep going."

While all this was going on at school, Amie was becoming more verbal at the foster home and was asking more questions about life. However, her foster parents were unable to give her any satisfactory answers. This was a difficult time for Amie because her body was changing and she was experiencing puberty. Amie did not understood what was happening to her during these changes. She remembers asking Flora about menstruation, and not much information was given verbally.

> "I was given a book from the agency, and just looked at the pictures because I couldn't read well. I tried to figure it out. But when I asked Flora, I think she was embarrassed to talk about it. I asked her again what area of the body 'it' came from. She said it was in the front. That was it."

It was time to wait. Her daughters knew about it, and even experienced it, but did not talk about it. It turned out that Amie got "it" in the spring of that year.

> "It would have been helpful for someone to talk to me about the changes I was experiencing, and tell me that it was a normal part of growing up; that menstruating was a part of becoming a young woman. I needed to wear a bra, but was given one that didn't fit. It was too big. The sanitary packet I was given explained how to wear a sanitary belt with a pad. Yet like with everything else, I was left to figure it out myself. I was so uncomfortable and felt exposed going to school with this new thing on. This was one more hurdle to contend with and felt so unlovely."

Amie remembered that she bled through her clothes and did not know what to do. "I was so embarrassed and ashamed because I couldn't do anything about it. I felt really yuckie. Bathing was reserved for weekends only," she recalled.

> "I was becoming more self-conscious about how I looked. All the other girls wore stylish clothes, makeup and curled-up hair with headbands while I was dressed in hand-me-downs in everything except underwear and shoes. Flora was able to sew and would cut down her daughter's clothes to make them fit me. I was still taken to the barber shop for boy haircuts, and felt like one too!"

Amie felt they did not want to deal with who she was becoming — a young woman. She finally realized in her heart they really did not really care about her, the way she wanted them to, and that taking care of her was just a job for them. "I never was told that I was pretty," she sadly recalls.

"I was given a bag lunch and everyone else got school lunch and snack money. I was afraid to ask for anything, because I didn't think they would give it to me."

When the students were done eating lunch, the lunch monitor would announce, "It's time to buy snacks." Amie was left watching most of her peers buy treats like ice cream sandwiches, chips or extra milk. "I sat there feeling awful, and was mad watching and wishing to be like my other classmates." Amie remembers no one offered to share with her and this made her feel left out again. This was a recurring pattern.

What happened next was the first and last time Amie "acted out" with this family. She decided to take spare change from the foster mother's wallet for snacks. It started out in small amounts, like nickels, dimes and quarters; nothing that anyone

would notice, really. However, by the time she was found out she was taking bigger amounts, like single dollar bills in order to cover the costs of the snacks she wanted at school. The foster family was in shock. Their teenage daughter screamed at Amie, "How dare you do this to my mother!" and took it upon herself to slap Amie across the face.

Amie says that Flora was so hurt that she laid on the couch for at least two days in anguish and it seemed to break her heart. When she calmed down, she approached Amie and asked her why she had done it. Amie told her, "I know that I was wrong, but I really wanted to be like the other kids in school." Flora just didn't understand. She felt like I betrayed her. Amie, being insightful, knew deep down inside that this hurt Flora most of all. Yet she had such a difficult time with always being treated differently from Flora's own children. This was her way of saying, "I've had enough! I know the difference. I want to be included, and treated like everyone else." Flora tried to tell Amie that she would have given her the allowance that the agency gave for that purpose, if Amie had only asked. Amie really did not believe her, and why should she? It had never been offered, even though she knew it was available for her. She exclaimed, "I wanted it to come from you!" Flora was so taken back and surprised by Amie's realization. It was very difficult for the Flora to accept her true feelings. From her perspective, she was doing the right thing, so why would this child go against her? However, in Amie's mind she did it because of that difference. She did not want to be treated as a second class citizen any more. No one ever discussed things with her to help her understand life. She had been talked at without any regard to her feelings, and her questions were never welcomed.

The longing for the foster parents to give her something from themselves was never realized. She tells me:

"There is no excuse for stealing, and for that I am truly sorry. I felt guilty for a long time. My heart ached for Flora because she never had the insight to understand what I was going through. I guess it was easier for her to take care of infants than a teenager like me. Even so, I loved her the most and still do."

As it turned out, this was the straw that broke the camel's back. The foster kids were all put to bed, and Amie could hear the conversation the foster family was having behind closed doors. She struggled to quietly move to the end of her bed she could hear all they were saying as she pressed her ear against the bedroom door.

"The discussion got louder and louder. Their children were really angry with me. 'Mom, Amie doesn't appreciate all you did for her! You have to stop being foster parents right now!' Oh boy, was I in trouble. I thought that they were going to kick me out that night! Jack interjected and said, 'Your mother will have to go out and get a regular job instead of working at home. Up until now she has been able to take care of everybody and help with the family expenses. Are you really ready for that kind of change?' Their children didn't seem to care. They were hurt for their mother's sake. The discussion went back and forth for a while, and then it was decided to let all the foster children go."

Looking back, Amie came to realize that the foster family were unable to really to understand what a foster child is missing

emotionally. Since a child in foster care is not living with his own family, the whole point of being placed in a foster family setting is to provide a substitute family. Each of us has a basic need to belong to someone. A foster child needs to feel that he is valued the same way that biological children are valued. When there is a separation between what is theirs and what is not, it is very damaging to someone living through the foster care system. The emotional trauma foster children go through by being separated from their own families and not being taken in emotionally by a foster family reinforces feelings of rejection. In the end, Amie and her foster family were hurt, and they were not able to get past it.

Following this incident, Flora, with regret, and through the urging of her family told the agency that Amie was not happy living in their home. She also told the social worker that she and her husband did not want to be foster parents anymore, and that they were making plans to move to Florida. As Amie shared this with me she said:

> "I felt really guilty for the other foster kids. It's true that I wasn't happy, but I really wanted to stay with them. I was very sad and confused as to why the Flora was willing to give us up so easily. She was all we knew. I hoped I could have changed her mind. She meant something very special to me, and I loved her as if she were my real mother. I cried inside myself, keeping my feelings all bottled up."

Tragically, the sad news is that none of these more positive feelings could have been expressed for a better outcome.

"The day had come for all of us to leave the foster home. Goodbyes were said, and Flora cried as each child left. When it was my turn to leave, Flora, Jack and one of their daughters gave me a tearful goodbye and walked out, shutting the front door behind them. I was left alone in the house with their eldest daughter until the agency driver came to pick me up and take me to the new foster home. When the driver arrived to take me away, I cried when I got into the car. The sun was shining, but my heart was broken. The morning was heart-wrenching for all of us, and I was worried about where the others would go. As we drove away from the house, I really didn't believe that Flora wanted to give us up in her hearts. She was very kind to us. She cared for us and I found comfort in her. This was the first time I saw her cry for us. She must have been attached to us on a deeper level."

It never occurred to Amie until that day that Flora's dedication to her and the other foster children showed that she really loved them, not by words, but by deeds.

Amie did not know what to expect from the new foster family, or what they were told. All she knew was that they lived an hour away, and they liked being foster parents.

LAST FOSTER CARE HOME

When Amie finally arrived in her new foster home, still a bit nervous, she found this new family was very friendly and welcomed her. "I was surprised by such a welcome!" she tells me. This was such contrast to what Amie experienced from the other foster home. "I really didn't know what to do with it or how to respond. Were they for real? I never felt this kind of kindness before," Amie shared with a smile. She remembers thinking, "Maybe this place would be okay." She went on to relate:

> "The family had one grown-up daughter of their own, a set of foster twins — a boy and a girl — and now me. Both foster parents were warm, open and relaxed. They were a close-knit family. The foster father had a job in the city, and his wife was a stay-at-home mom. Nothing in their home was off-limits for us. They shared everything they had, even the *refrigerator*. I was free; I could eat. I gained twenty pounds living there and am still trying to take off the last ten all these years later. The truth is that this was such a comfort to me, and I felt like this was what a normal family does."

Daily life for Amie was different and everything was done as a family.

> "Unlike the other foster home, we all sat down and watched television after dinner. The atmosphere was much calmer; I could be myself. I felt like I had been in prison, and someone had let me out. I was given lunch money. The foster mother took me shopping and I learned how to wear makeup. I even had a cake on my birthday. The foster mother took great care of me during that "time of the month." She used to refer to it as "Being on well." She explained everything. She nursed me back to health when life was difficult. She treated me like a daughter, not a foster child. I felt like I was part of their family."

This was the family Amie was wishing for all these years. Sadly, all of the foster mother's efforts of kindness to reach out were not understood. Amie was still grieving over the other foster family. She missed Christmas and Easter and struggled to fit in.

> "I couldn't understand what this Hanukah was all about — one gift a night?! For Christmas everybody got their gifts all at once. Isn't that a better idea? I may have not gotten as many presents as the other foster family's kids did, but the whole community looked forward to it, and so did I. They decorated a tree with lights and it was so pretty. When Easter came around, why did this family celebrate Passover? I had no clue what that meant. Where were the Easter bunny baskets and

candy? Who cared about Matzo? And besides, I felt like if I joined in on the Jewish holidays, I was going behind the Italian foster family's back."

This foster family really did try hard to include Amie in their lives, but it did not quite work.

"I just didn't fit in, even though I wished I could. I felt bad that I was hurting them by rejecting their attempts, but what else could I do? I really didn't understand their goodness. It felt wrong. They tried to give me a sense of value, but I guess I was jaded by the other foster family. They did plant good seeds and I felt that they were really good people for a child who really needed them. I think their family was what a foster family was supposed to be. They left me with good memories."

By the end of middle school, the agency decided Amie needed to be placed into a group home.

"It was explained to me that the group home was designed for girls in situations like mine. It was a home for girls that came from their biological families, or from other foster homes. They didn't fit in anywhere else. Each girl would be treated as an individual and that gave us each a chance for success. What made it a clincher for me was that the house parent in charge of the girls' care was Italian. That was it. It made this move okay by me. I was really looking forward to it."

Amie felt as though she was becoming an individual with her own ideas. Amie was finally heard, and made aware of the kind of place she was heading to next.

THE GROUP HOME YEARS

It was again time for Amie to go to summer sleep-away camp. This would be her last time. During this stay, Amie tried to learn how to swim. The problem was that her legs could not reach the top of the water and neither could her arms. She told me all she could do was the "doggie paddle" and float on her back like a lump.

> "The sun was always in my eyes. I could jump into the deep water but barely caught my breath coming up. Thankfully, there was always a spotter there to help me out. I sure needed it. I really had a good time that summer. I didn't feel that those in charge wanted to get rid of me, so it was fun."

When sleep-away camp was over, it was time for a new adventure. Amie was going to live in the city, meet new people and learn new things. This placement would play an important role in her future. To Amie's happy surprise, the group home was named Friendly Home for Girls. The agency operated two of them located in the city within ten blocks of each other.

> "I was thirteen and three quarters and going into ninth grade when I arrived at the home. The

house parent, Mazie, said to me, 'I knew these things were yours, because I saw the small shoes. I am surprised that you only have one small square box of clothing.' I was about to start my first year of high school. Wow, that was something! I was going to be fourteen in October, had no idea what to expect, but I was glad to be there."

All of the girls were on the same playing field, so to speak. There were eight of them in total. There were two girls in each bedroom, and everyone shared the bathroom at the end of the long hallway. The girls ranged in age from fourteen through eighteen years old. After the age of eighteen, and once finished with high school, each girl would be discharged from the agency. However, if any one of them decided to attend college, she would remain under the agency's jurisdiction up to twenty-two years of age.

One of the first things Amie learned was that the group home was known as the "group residence." All of the girls came to identify it as this. Secondly, she learned that there were house rules that each girl had to follow in order to live there. These included keeping their space in the bedrooms clean, rotating the kitchen chores, and taking a shower every night, as well as doing their our own laundry.

It took Amie a while to learn the rules of the residence and the chores that came with it.

"I had no experience cleaning, doing kitchen chores, washing my own clothes, or taking a shower every day. Mazie had to teach me how to do these things. The first thing she taught me was the value of taking a shower every day. Mazie believed that being clean helped us girls feel better

about ourselves, especially around that "time of the month." With eight teenage girls living in the house, keeping clean was an important part of staying healthy. Mazie was right. It seemed like every girl had it, every week of the month. What drama! Mazie would say, 'I want my girls to be clean in mind and body.' I wasn't good at it at first, and was frustrated easily. After dinner and clean up, the production of getting ready for the next day started. All the girls had to have their showers done by ten o'clock at night. That was a sight to see. If someone was in the shower too long, an argument would break out and Mazie would have to bang on the bathroom door in order to keep the line moving. "Time's up! Next..." Mazie would shout. It was a real frenzy, but we all managed to get our showers in before lights out every night."

Amie continued:

"I remember my roommate trying to show me how to keep my side of the room, and found myself crying a lot because I couldn't keep it up. Sometimes we would fight over it, and then Mazie would have to be the referee. She always sent me back to my room to work it out with my roommate, Jane. She did this for the other girls as well. I was sloppy, and Jane wasn't. I became a real clutter bug. This was the first time I had things that I could keep! So when it got out of control, I didn't know what to get rid of because

it reminded me of things being taken away. What was I supposed to keep? I had no clue."

Amie's clutter became her treasure. She was emotionally attached to everything and really had to be convinced that some things should be either given away or thrown away. It was especially difficult if something had been broken because she was afraid that she could never replace it. For Amie, being attached to things became more important than being attached to people. She really was not attached to anyone at this stage in her life, making it difficult for her to know the difference.

"Yet it was difficult for me to let go of the Italian foster family, especially when the holidays came around and the other girls left the residence to visit their families. One of those days, I decided to call their house to see if they really moved. I missed them and wanted to know. The residence had a pay phone in a closet for the girls to use for personal calls. This closet was very small, and the pay phone was mounted on the opposite wall. There was a bench to sit on the other wall. We could close the door to the closet for privacy. I missed the family and wanted to know if they had gone. When the foster mother picked up the phone I hung up quickly. I didn't want them to know it was me. It seemed to me that they had lied about moving to Florida and were still in town."

At the residence, dinner time was set in stone. The food was cooked by the houseparent on duty every day. Amie explained:

"It was scheduled for six o'clock in the evening every weeknight unless one of us had to be out of the house for an after school activity or a job that required us to be there. On the weekends, dinner was up for grabs. Mazie ate dinner with us and encouraged us to talk about our day, and she would also inform us of any changes that the social worker might have regarding meetings with her."

After dinner, every girl had to take her turn clearing the table and doing the dishes.

"A rotating schedule was put on the kitchen wall so that each of us knew whose turn it was to do the kitchen chores. I didn't have trouble setting the table or clearing it after dinner, but doing the dishes was another story. The dishes and the pots had to be stacked in such a way so that they could be washed by hand. There was no dishwasher available and it was such a boring job. None of us liked doing it, and we tried to negotiate our way out of it. We all had good excuses, but ended up doing it anyway. I tried not to volunteer for anyone. My turn was enough for me. Mazie would have to sit in the kitchen with me to make sure I did it. Much of the time I would have a temper tantrum, yelling, 'I can't do this!' By the time I finally finished the job, an hour later, I would be covered from my belly to my toes in dish water and a little puddle would be in front of my feet. Mazie would say, 'I should get you a rubber apron.' But she never got me one. Mazie

always reminded me, 'You are just like anyone else. And whatever you put your mind to do, you can do it. I will not put limits on you!' Kitchen chores were part of keeping a clean house. Mazie believed in hard work and I trusted her, even though I would get soaking wet."

Mazie never allowed Amie to feel sorry for herself because of her disability. She never wanted Amie to use that as an excuse.

This was the first time in Amie's life that she would be responsible for doing her own laundry. Amie had a little bit of knowledge about doing laundry because she watched the foster mothers doing the wash. The powdered laundry soap was in a big box and placed by the washing machine in the utility room off the kitchen. The Spic and Span floor cleaner was also a powder in a box the same size as the laundry detergent, and was placed right next to the laundry detergent.

"No one did laundry for us and it was up to me to keep our clothes clean. It didn't take me long to get the hang of it. One morning after getting my outfit ready for school, as I put on one of my old dresses with matching tights, I felt that I had accomplished something by getting my clothes washed and myself prepared. But when I got to school, all of a sudden I began to scratch my legs, then my arms, then my chest. I was so itchy and I didn't know why.
By the end of the school day I was covered with hives. It took me over an hour to get back to the residence. I couldn't take the scratching anymore and I wanted to rip my clothes off. After I finally changed my clothes, I told Mazie what happened,

and showed her the hives. She walked me over
to the two boxes of powder next to the washer,
laughing while she scooping the Spic and Span,
saying, 'You scooped the wrong one!' I felt silly
and embarrassed. I never did that again. Mazie
and I had a good laugh over it."

Mazie exposed Amie to supermarkets, restaurants and other
kind of stores which, believe it or not, she had never experi-
enced before while living with the foster families. The local
supermarket was only a couple of blocks away from the resi-
dence. Mazie would send Amie to buy small amounts of food
when they would run out of something. She did not want her
to carry heavy bags of food back, so she made her a small shop-
ping list. Mazie made sure that all of the girls did some food
shopping in order to teach them what the food really cost and
so that they could learn to stick to a budget.

"This was such an eye-opener for me. There was
so much food to choose from. I didn't know that
so much food existed. There was also a specialty
store next to the supermarket called Zabar's. It
was a gourmet kosher store that was famous for
their bagels, cheeses, meats, lox, condiments and
sandwiches. There was also a Carvel ice cream
store located on the same avenue as the super-
market. I spent a lot of time there, and it was my
favorite place, even though I gained ten pounds."

There was never any pressure for any of the girls to go on
a diet. All meals were provided, including dessert, which was
usually an Entenmann's cake.

"Most evenings we drank a large cup of tea and watched television, because there were no snacks in the house. Because I gained ten pounds I started having trouble walking. Mazie noticed this and suggested, 'Will you trust me if you only eat what I tell you to eat?' I told her 'Okay.' She made sure that I ate a small breakfast, and had a piece of fruit with lunch. I was not allowed to buy snacks at school, and there was no dessert at dinner. She was a hawk! It took at least three months to lose the weight and I did feel better. It didn't stay off for long, but nevertheless it was a good try."

The agency had a policy of giving each girl a clothing allowance of $300 per year, with half of it being given at one time during the year, and the other half later in the year. "I thought that was a lot of money. I had always worn hand–me- downs, and now I had the chance to buy my own clothes." Half the money went for fall and winter clothes, and the other half went for spring and summer clothes. "I got an additional amount for orthopedic shoes, one pair twice a year. Mazie told me if I wanted or needed something more, I would have to work for it. But why would I have to? That was so much money. Would that be enough?"

Mazie thought it would be a good idea to take Amie shopping for her first winter coat.

"I tried on a number of them and Mazie told me which ones looked good on me. We both liked one particular coat. It was a brown coat with gold-toned buttons. Mazie paid for it in cash. There weren't any credit cards or checks used back then.

'This was a good first outing,' Mazie told me."

Next time I'd be going out on my own with all that cash.

"I was so glad that Mazie took me to get that coat. Now I had to go out and shop for myself. I decided to go to the same store I had went with Mazie. There was so much to look at, and so many people around the store. It had three floors of merchandise, and you had to use an escalator to get on the upper floors. Mazie took me to the junior department, so I thought that would be a good place to start looking for my new clothes. Once I got there, I noticed a display of warm looking turtlenecks in all fall colors. As I was looking through all the colors and sizes, I found one, a green and brown flowered print I liked. I picked it up, and raised it up high to see if it would fit me. After taking a good look at it, it seemed like it would fit. '*That's good*,' I thought. Then, as I was about to look at another display, I noticed that my purse was gone. I panicked. I looked through the turtleneck display again to see if the purse was under something, and I couldn't find it. 'Oh, no ...the money is gone!' I cried. All I could think of was that I was gonna get in trouble for losing the money. I didn't know what to do. I must have looked for the purse for a good half hour, and then realized it was really gone. It was a good thing I found a subway token in the coat that Mazie and I had picked out so I could get back to the residence. I left the store in tears and cried all the way back. Mazie was there to greet me at the door and

asked, 'What happened?' My voice was shaking, my words whimpering and drawn out, and my eyes being full of tears. I explained everything to her. She listened to my story, and when I stopped crying she said, 'Amie from now on, you mustn't ever let go of your purse. You have to keep it in your hands at all times. When you want to look at something, you can only use one hand. I'm sorry that this happened to you, but I bet it will never happen again.' I had to wear what I had on hand. Mazie felt sorry for me, but encouraged me again saying, 'You will have another chance when it is time to buy your spring clothes.' So, the next time I went out shopping with her help, I didn't leave my purse anywhere but in my hand."

Mazie decided to take Amie out to lunch after they finished shopping. This was something Mazie would do with the other girls as well. This was an opportunity for Mazie to share time with each girl time to talk about things. Mazie always referred to the girls as "her girls," and she really enjoyed spending time with them. "Mazie said to me, 'Little One, what's going on with you?' The name stuck and she always called me that because she said my shoes were so small. I liked that name and besides I wasn't that tall anyway. So the shoe fit!"

As they talked and ate their lunch, Mazie shared her own life story with Amie, and told her:

"As a young woman I was a union organizer, and involved with liberal politics. I never thought that I would get married until I met my husband at a union meeting. He was very smitten with me. It was only after we were married that he

told me that he couldn't have any children; but I told him, 'Well, you never tried to have any with me!' Within our first two years we had our little girl. My heart was broken when my husband died of cancer when our baby was only two years old. Due to my job, I wasn't able to be home much with our daughter, so my mother watched her while I was working. Every night, I would come home after she was sleeping and watch her sleep, and moved her little things. I wanted to make sure she knew that I was there."

Amie said that Mazie and her daughter were very close.

School attendance was mandatory. There were three high schools used by the agency, two of which were close to the residence. Each of the schools had special programs, such as nursing, preliminary studies, or college programs to suit the girls' needs and prepare them for adult life. Mazie and the social worker decided that the best school for Amie would be the one on the other side of town, because the school had an elevator; but this meant Amie would have to travel. She did not have any real experience with public transportation, especially on her own. Mazie said to Amie:

"Let's go on the bus to your school and meet your guidance counselor. I want to see if you if you can maneuver around the school safely, and if you can manage to take the bus. I think that this school is the best option for you and my main concern is that you don't fall. All we need are a bunch of students bumping into you, and down you go."

Amie went onto relate:

"I felt really felt special and important to Mazie because she took the time with me to make sure I was safe. She didn't do that with any of the other girls. When we got back to the residence, Mazie said, 'This worked for you! You should only travel on the bus. Please don't take the subway so I don't worry about you falling. There are more people on the subway train than there are on the bus. You won't have to worry about so many stairs going on the bus, either. It is long walk down the steps into the subway to catch a train, and you have to make sure that you are fast enough to get it. I don't want you rushing. Besides, the walk to the bus is shorter.'"

Mazie was right. Taking the bus was easier for Amie.

"I liked the way I was treated on the bus. The bus driver would always wait to move until I was seated; and when I got off, he would always make sure that I got off safely. I was able to hold on better to the strap hangers because the bus did not go as fast as the train. That made it easier for me to travel and get around to other places besides school. I went to individual therapy sessions, met with my social worker, attended appointments for physical exams, saw the agency doctor, and went back and forth to different part-time jobs I had. Back then, gold plated tokens with the emblem of the city were sold for fifty cents apiece. No real change was ever used and one token was used per ride. We all had monthly bus passes for school. For most trips, I needed to take two buses. This

meant I would need to transfer from one to the other. Usually, I would get a free transfer ticket to get on the other bus. The agency was on the other side of town and occasionally we girls would take a taxi back if the group meetings ran late. I managed to learn how to use the subway. It was a job and I had to work at it. I had to make sure that I carried my purse and backpack and held on to the banister to get down the stairs in one piece. Most of the time when I finally got down to the stairs, I missed the train and had to wait for another one. The only thing good about it was that I could get to places faster."

It was time for the school year to begin and Amie remembers how anxious she was.

"Going to high school made me a little nervous. I didn't know what to expect. With everyone changing classes for each subject, and having my own locker, I felt intimidated at the size of it all. It was a large, three story building in a bigger part of the city, and many more students to deal with. I wondered how the students and teachers would react to my disability. I was able to use the building elevator to get from class to class. The guidance counselor thought that I would do well in a special program called College Bound Students. It gave me the opportunity for individual attention in my studies and it kept me on track."

This program worked out well for Amie, except that she was never satisfied with the low to mid-seventies grade point average. Amie told me:

> "I tried to study, and spend more time doing homework more than any of the girls in the residence. I never saw them doing much homework. Reading was so difficult and I didn't remember what I read. Still, I was allowed to stay in the program because my grades were passing. I was still frustrated with all the work I had to do to keep these grades. I was afraid of failing."

Amie's favorite thing was to be able was able to participate in the music program. She learned to play the flute and violin and took voice lessons, which allowed her to sing with the school chorus. "No one at the residence complained about me practicing these instruments. Taking voice lessons was my favorite. The teacher was a professional singer, and really enjoyed teaching his students. Singing made me happy, and I really felt good about myself."

As time went on, Amie came to admire her roommate, Jane. She was very clean, well-organized, and she was a beautiful girl. Her mother was Jewish, and her father was Filipino. She resembled her father. Just like Amie, Jane came from a foster family before coming to the group residence.

> "Jane confided in me that she was sexually abused by one of the sons in the foster home she lived in. When she told the foster parents about it, the foster parents made her leave. That was the real reason Jane was placed in the group residence. I never heard of this before and I felt sad for

her. I told her, 'Why would anyone do that? It's not right!'

Jane then said, 'I see you as my little sister, Amie.' She still does!"

The two became very close, even though Jane was two years older than Amie. They still keep in touch to this very day.

Amie went on to say:

> "One day I was walking on a main street in the city and I came across a deli, and walked in. All of a sudden I noticed someone I knew behind the counter wearing a cook's apron, making food. It was the foster father from the home I lived in before the residence. He recognized me and wanted to know how I was doing. We were very glad to see each other, and he invited me to sit down and chat while he made me a sandwich. We talked for a while, and I told him that I was still in high school. He mentioned that the foster children still in their care were doing well. His wife and daughter were doing fine. After I finished my sandwich, I got up and said good-bye to him. I gave him a big hug, and he wished me all the best."

Amie later found out that this foster father had suffered a severe heart attack, and had passed away. The foster mother in turn had to give up being a foster mother. Amie never found out what happened to their family and felt very sad, saying, "They were good people, and he was a very kind and loving man. My time with him at the deli is something that I will never forget. I didn't realize saying good-bye would be forever."

Amie then went on to discuss another experience:

"I had finished the tenth grade and took the Algebra Regents twice before finally passing it. Now it was time to move on to the third year of high school. My guidance counselor asked to see me. She was a very caring and lovely lady. She always wore a pretty dress, low heels and had her hair in a French knot. She was very approachable. When I went to her office, she let me know there was a program available that would help me in reading and math. It was created for low income students who wanted to go to college even though their grades were low. I definitely qualified for that, big time. I was to go to a hospital on the east side of town every Saturday morning during the school year for extra help. It just so happened to be in the same hospital where I had had my heel cord surgeries. What a coincidence! In the summer time, they provided work opportunities in different departments in their outpatient clinics at the hospital. A pink uniform was provided for the girls. It looked like a nurse's uniform with snaps in the front. The guys wore white pants, a white shirt and a tie color of their choice. We received a stipend for our work. I worked in the Outpatient Diabetic Clinic, and stayed with the program until I graduated high school."

It was through this opportunity that Amie met a wonderful, strong, beautiful -- and tall — woman whose name was Kellie. Kellie was a nurse and educator who took vows in the Catholic Church, and worked as a missionary to the Bolivian people in South America. She put away her nun's habit after twenty years to pursue helping at-risk adolescents in the city, while keeping

her Catholic faith. Kellie was the director of the program at the hospital, and Amie felt a connection to her right away. Kellie was drawn to Amie as well and she had a real impact on her.

Amie drew confidence from the attention and dignity Kellie gave to her. "It was through Kellie I got the drive to pursue the possibility of going to college. She was a strong woman, from strong stock, and treated us with great respect. I always knew what to expect from her, and she taught me how to be self-reliant."

A few years after Amie graduated from high school, she learned that Kellie had left the program, and moved to another state. There, she had become a foster parent of at-risk children, and eventually married her college sweetheart. Amie was able to keep in touch with her over the phone and through occasional visits throughout the years.

> "I really admired and respected Kellie. She had similar qualities to Mazie. I felt very comfortable around her. She helped me explore ideas and focus on what I could accomplish with my life. She had the ability to give to others with high expectations. Kellie believed that each of us was responsible for our own choices, and that it was normal to make mistakes that could be fixed."

Mazie put a high priority on the value of working. She wanted these experiences to be positive in nature, and monitored as to which ones would be best for each girl. She believed that learning how to work was part of the process of becoming a self-sufficient, independent person. The jobs she encouraged the girls to take on were babysitting, working in a store, tutoring, and working in the school library.

"One of my first jobs was a babysitting job. It was a big deal; I had never done that before. The girl that was supposed to do it couldn't make it, so Mazie asked if I would be willing to try. She called up the parents were willing to have me do the job. They said 'yes.' I was so glad, but nervous too. The going rate was only two dollars and fifty cents per hour. That was a lot of cash for me."

That was a lot of money back then, and there were many baby-sitting jobs that followed for Amie. The girls were not allowed to be out of the house past 10:00 at night during the weeknights. It was the family's responsibility to get the babysitters back to the residence by cab.

"Most of us worked on New Year's Eve and made a big twenty dollars for the night. Another job that I had in high school was putting away books in the school library. This job was convenient for me because I didn't have to travel after school."

Amie was able to use the skills from this job later on for another library job.

Amie liked living in the group residence. Not all the girls living there shared Amie's enthusiasm. Most of the girls felt turned away from their families and often struggled with self-identity; the hardest of their struggles was that they had to sort out their personal issues with their dysfunctional family situations without enough support. "You had to behave like a grown up, before you were really ready to be one. I didn't have a family to go back home to. For me this was my focus, to have a real future." Living in the group residence with Mazie fostered the confidence and reassurance to explore life's options. Amie learned what it meant to

discover and grow into who she was and wanted to be. This is part of being an adolescent. "Mazie taught me about self-acceptance, trustworthiness, and love. She was a strong woman, yet approachable and reliable. She was my cheerleader, and a real parent to me, and had a great influence on my life. She gave me her heart and soul."

The focus of living in the group residence for Amie and the other girls was on placement adjustment. That meant that the girls were guided to focus on living together by following resident rules and completing high school. The agency provided support to keep this focus through required weekly individual and group therapy sessions with the social worker.

> "There wasn't much talk in how to function in the outside world, though. Mazie was the only one who tried to instill in all of us that we were capable of having successful lives. She seemed to know how hard it would be to adjust to living on our own, with so many emotional issues to deal with. Many times these issues interfered with making sound decisions. There was no "home" to go back to if things got overwhelming, or out of hand. Neither was there any real support system to rely on. Mazie was all we had."

Her help proved to be very crucial in the coming months when real life decisions were going to be made before Amie would leave the residence.

Most of Amie's time living in the group residence was a positive experience. The only times it was difficult for her was during the holiday seasons. Amie noticed that a few of the girls would go and spend time with their biological families.

"I wanted to go with them. After I turned seventeen, just before Christmas I made a call and contacted the Italian foster family. I wasn't sure how they would react to my phone call. I told them that I was living in the city in a group residence and persuaded them to let me come and see them. I also asked if my roommate Jane could come with me, because she didn't have anywhere to go on Christmas Day. They kind of agreed and let her come along. I was so excited that I was going to see them. I wanted them to be proud of how far I had come since I left their home. I wanted them to meet my best friend, too. A bit strange, right? Jane and I took the train to their town and were picked up by one of their daughters. I was treated cordially, but more like an acquaintance than someone who lived in their home for ten years. They acted as if nothing ever happened. There was no discussion of what took place in the past. Maybe that was an improvement...They seemed glad that Jane and I were doing well. I had hoped that this visit would have been a stepping stone for a reconnection with them again. But the old stuff came back to in my mind, and I felt empty. They didn't invite us back as we said our goodbyes. After we boarded on the train, Jane and I talked about feeling a bit sad. This turned out to be just a visit and nothing more. It would have to be up to me to make a life somehow for myself, and Jane and I made a promise that we would be each other's support as long as we lived."

FINDING OUT WHERE
SHE CAME FROM

Amie's visit to the Italian foster family that Christmas gave her the courage to find out where she came from. Her anxious mind wondered:

> "Did I have any family? Would they want to know who I was? Should I really do this? I thought that maybe finding my family would help bring a sense of belonging somehow. The real question was, 'What would I find?' I discussed this idea with Mazie, of course. She thought it was an excellent idea. She told me over and over again that it was better knowing the truth about something, rather than wondering about it or believing a lie, or worrying about something that could never happen. Mazie suggested that I talk it over with the social worker to see if she could find out anything about my back ground."

Over the course of the next few months, the social worker came up with a lot of information, and wanted Mazie to work

with Amie to prepare her for what she was about to learn about her family.

> "Truth be told, it turned out that Mazie's hands were tied because she was instructed to only say certain things to me by the social worker. Mazie knew everything that was discovered, but she was not allowed to tell me directly what the truth was. The social worker wanted to do it all; she wanted the glory. I remember Mazie telling me to be prepared for the worst. 'What could that be?' I wondered. Mazie would tell me things like, 'Maybe your birth mother is an alcoholic.' Could that be true? Why would that make her give me up? I really didn't have any idea what a real alcoholic was anyway. All I knew was what I saw in the movies. That made me feel sad, and I didn't like it. I even stayed away from drinking and smoking because I didn't think it was a good thing. Drugs were never mentioned. I didn't like that either. Mazie tried really hard to make me understand, but I just couldn't."

Amie finally had the meeting with the social worker where she would find out about her birth family. The social worker told Amie that her birth mother and father were heroin addicts. This was the reason her birth mother couldn't keep her. She had no means to support Amie.

> "When I first heard this I didn't believe it. How could this be? Mazie was telling me the truth all along! When I told her what the social worker said, she calmly told me, 'I know. I'm sorry, Amie.'

All I could do was cry. I cried for weeks. This was such a shock and there was more…It turned out that my birth mother had become a heroin addict as a result of being with my birth father. He was supposedly the one who had gotten her hooked on the drug in the first place. My birth mother was in and out of rehab centers, but nothing worked for her. She ended up being put on Methadone, a prescription heroin substitute."

The social worker then went on to say that Amie's birth mother came from a struggling middle class family of Jewish immigrants from Manchester, England. When they came to the United States, a few of their relatives came along with them. Amie's birth family settled in one of uptown boroughs of the city. Amie's grandfather was a taxi cab driver, and her grandmother was a homemaker. Amie's birthmother was the middle child of three children. She had an older sister and a younger brother.

"The social worker told me that my birth mother's family tried really hard to help her. They were so devastated by her unplanned pregnancy, and when her father heard the news that she was pregnant he had a heart attack. Both of my grandparents died fairly young, in their early sixties. I never met them.

She went on to tell me that my birth mother's older sister reached out to help her the most. Eight years after I was born, my birth mother met another man and gave birth to twin girls. Like me, they were born prematurely, at around the six months' gestation. After a while, the doctors

noticed that one of the twins was not developing normally. My birth mother was not able to take care of the girls properly because she was still on heroin when they were born. By the time the twins were eighteen months old, before my grandmother died, she asked her eldest daughter if she would be willing to take the 'healthy' twin, her niece, to live with her family. She wanted this child to have the opportunity for a normal life. Her eldest daughter did as her mother requested and raised her as if she was her own child, along with her three other children."

The severely disabled twin, who needed twenty-four hour care, was diagnosed with cerebral palsy and mental retardation. She stayed with our birth mother while bound to a wheelchair. I heard that this gave my birthmother a renewed focus to clean up her act so that Child Protective Services wouldn't take her away from her."

"This news was so overwhelming to me. What's more, my birth mother had been living only ten blocks away from the residence while I was living there, before she moved to a low income project uptown. That was surreal by far. All my fears came upon me. I didn't want to accept it. The family I was hoping for didn't exist. I was so angry and upset. 'Why did this have to happen to me?' I asked myself. 'Was there anything else?' I wondered. It was really hard for me to take all of this in. I wanted to scream! How could she do this to me? How could she do this to herself? Once maybe, but twice? The social worker tried to smooth things over with me, but I was mad! I

just couldn't reason my way out of this. It didn't make any sense.

Mazie, of course, put things in proper perspective. She kept reminding me, 'Amie, even though this is a hard pill to swallow, you could overcome this by focusing on your success and making better choices. You are not responsible for what happened, nor should you be responsible for them in the future.' It felt like such a burden on my shoulders, since I was only seventeen at the time. I almost didn't want to go through with meeting them after finding all this out but, as usual, Mazie insisted. 'Amie, you have to meet them. Otherwise you will always wonder what they look like, and you have something to offer them.' I gave in and was so nervous, and didn't know how to react. I had no feelings for them because I didn't even know them. Mazie couldn't come with me to do this. I had to meet her by myself at the social worker's office. 'Oh God, help me!' I prayed."

"My birth mother was thrilled to meet me and see what I had become. My half-sister in the wheel chair was with her to greet me. My birth mother told me to call her Zelda, and gave me a big hug. The first thing she said—with tears in her eyes—was, 'You look just like your father.' She went on to tell me her life story. What a story it was."

Amie told me that it took a few months for the shock of it all to wear off. At the same time, the social worker arranged for bi-monthly meetings in her office for us to get to know each other.

"All I kept thinking was, 'This could have been me. I could have been the one in that wheelchair'. This could have turned out to be terrible for me. I felt awful. I didn't share any of this with the social worker or my birth mother. I only felt safe to talk about it with Mazie. I knew she understood.

During my individual therapy sessions with the social worker, I was told that the agency had a group home for disabled children. I thought that this might help my half-sister, who was twelve at the time. Maybe, there was a chance that she could walk, or something, I thought. When I told Zelda about it, she refused to sign the papers, and accused me, saying adamantly, 'You are taking my baby away from me. The answer is no!' I couldn't understand why she didn't want to make her daughter's life better. I thought that she was selfish. I tried to explain to her that maybe there was something that could have been done for her. But she insisted that since they didn't do anything up to now, it was too late. I didn't agree with her. But now I realize that she was defensive and didn't want to be alone. She couldn't get rid of her own guilt, and from then on she was so manipulative. She even tried to make me feel guilty by saying, 'That could have been you.' This fed on all my fears.

The only thing this did was cause me to be angry and frustrated. It seemed like she took her frustrations out on me. I even tried living with her for a short time to have some kind of relationship with her. She put me in a place of parenthood over her and my half-sister, and it became

overwhelming. After an awful summer with her, I said to myself, 'This is it; I have to leave.' I had hoped that we could have been friends on some level, but she wasn't able to do it. She couldn't be a mother or even a friend. She wasn't strong enough to be in my corner. The only feeling I came away with was feeling used. How sad for all of us. I was really hurting, and I handled things the best I could. I think she was jealous that I could have a future, and she was living in the past. She was always on my mind after I left her apartment, and I felt badly that I couldn't fix it. Mazie told me to hang in there, but it was too much. It took me over seven years of an on-and-off relationship to finally severe ties that were going nowhere. I finally had enough. I wrote my birth mother a letter saying I couldn't handle her situation any longer and she had to let me go. This was probably hard for her to hear from me, but deep down inside she probably knew it."

Sometime in the fall after Amie met her birth mother, she went in for her yearly physical examination downtown at the agency. The doctor consulted with an orthopedic surgeon and they decided Amie needed two more operations to gain more flexibility and stability for walking. These operations were similar to the heel-cord release operations she had undergone when she was twelve years old. They wanted to cut and stretch the muscles connected to each hip. "The idea of having to go through more operations made me anxious. I remembered the last one as a horrendous experience, and didn't want to go through it again."

A Real Spiritual Encounter

While Amie was waiting to find out when the operations were going to take place, one of her classmates approached her to tell her about her Christian faith.

> "We both were in the college-bound program in the same high school, and shared many classes together. Betty and I talked about our work load and she began to share her faith in Jesus with me. I wondered why Betty was sharing this part of her life with me. I didn't recall if I told her I was Jewish, and the way she talked about her faith intrigued me. Her Jesus was personal and approachable. He seemed very real to her, and wasn't the Jesus–as He had been portrayed to me –Who hated the Jews. Our conversations about her faith became more frequent as we spent more time together. She explained to me that believing in Jesus would impact my life for the better. One thing she said to me was, 'If you accept Jesus into your heart, he will heal you.' What a statement! That's all I needed to hear. I didn't want to go through another round of operations again."

Betty invited Amie to her Spanish church many times.

"I didn't understand a thing, but I liked being with my friend Betty, as well as the friendly people there. They would often invite me to Sunday dinners after church and took a real interest in me. Eventually, Betty's pastor got to know me and led me in the 'Sinners Prayer,' which went something like this: Dear Heavenly Father, I now understand that Jesus is Your one and only Son Who died for me on the cross, so I could have eternal life. Please forgive me of my sins, and help me follow You for the rest of my life. He also prayed with me for my physical healing."

Amie hoped that with this prayer, everything would change.

"I felt a burden lift off my shoulders, and a sense of acceptance. I felt like God would hear my prayers now, even with my disability. Yet my heart was set on a healing for my body, but that did not happen right away. At first I was quite amazed, as well as a bit confused. I even wondered if I was still Jewish, because Betty told me that I was now a Christian. That term seemed odd to me, because it made me think of the Italian foster home. Their being Christian was very different than the way Betty behaved as a Christian. We didn't really discuss it, but I knew that I was different on the inside after I prayed to receive Jesus into my heart."

Amie also said that she wasn't as anxious any more. After a while, the doctors decided that they were not going to do the

surgeries on Amie's hips because they felt that the end result would be that it would interfere with her ability to walk up and down stairs. When Amie heard this, she was so excited and relieved. This was a great answer to prayer.

Amie started going to a Bible study after school, and was inspired to read the New Testament for the first time in her life. The version she read was called the *Good News Bible*. "I was so surprised that I could read it or even understand it. Gradually, I learned some Bible verses that were very comforting. Betty was there for me when I had questions. My eyes were opened and things began to make sense to me."

One day, Amie decided that it was time to share her experience with Mazie.

> "Mazie handled it quite well, considering she was an atheist. She did seem surprised, and felt the need to share this with the social worker because, after all, it was a Jewish agency. At first they weren't too pleased, and were concerned that I had joined a cult. I began to wonder if I would be allowed to stay in the residence. It was touchy for a while, so Betty and I prayed that I would be able to stay there. When the shock wore off, the social worker told me I could stay as long as I didn't try to make other girls Christians, too. Our prayers were answered."

Amie did have a desire to share her new faith with the other girls, but made sure she didn't pressure them to believe. "I just wanted to share my experiences with them, because I cared about what was happening in their lives." This gave Amie more confidence that she had a purpose for her life that she did not have before. "I spent more time with Betty and her family until

the school year was over. We stayed in touch with her for a couple of years, until Betty moved away."

It was during this time that Amie accidently came upon a place where Jewish people who believed in Jesus met for fellowship. It was close to the residence, and she could even walk there. The name of this congregation was Beth Sar Shalom, which meant "House of the Prince of Peace." It was a mission outreach organization focused on bringing Jesus (*Yeshua* in Hebrew) to the Jewish people. (Subsequently, there was a name change and it is now called Chosen People Ministries.)

The history of this kind of congregation began way back in the late 1800s. It was started by an Orthodox Jewish rabbi named Leopold Cohn from Hungary, who was studying the Hebrew Scriptures and reading the Old Testament prophets. He began to study the Book of Isaiah, and saw that in Chapter 53, it described what the Messiah was supposed to do.

As a young person, around age seven, Leopold Cohn lost his parents and began to trust in his God for help because he was all alone. When he was Bar Mitzvah age, thirteen, he decided that he would study the Torah and become a rabbi. He married and was a happy man, always looking for the Messiah. He did an in-depth study about when the Messiah was supposed to come and explored this idea, researching the book of Daniel in the Old Testament. He also studied the Talmud, which Orthodox Jews believe to be the oral law. Eventually, he found himself questioning whether or not the Messiah had come. This spiritual search ended for him during the Chanukah festival of lights. His fellow rabbis did not appreciate his searching and persecuted him for it.

By 1892 he made the move to go to America, because he thought it would give him the freedom he needed to pursue his quest, since America was the land where one could go to find freedom from religious persecution. Once in America, he made

his way to New York City. He fell upon a church that had meetings called "meetings for Jews," which piqued his interest. He met with the minister, who also happened to be Jewish. He told him how he had searched the Scriptures and had discovered how Jesus was the Messiah. This man gave Rabbi Cohn a New Testament in Hebrew for him to read. He gladly accepted this New Testament and began to read it. He had so many questions about how a Jew could believe in this Jesus of the Gentiles. He kept hearing in his heart that no matter what those Gentiles did in the name of Jesus, he would have to follow him if He indeed were the Messiah.

More Scriptures were opened to him as he searched, and the time came when he realized that Jesus was indeed the Messiah, and decided to commit his life to Him. As a result of his decision, fellow Jews considered him to be a traitor to his people. When his former colleagues wrote to his wife — who was not with him — and informed her of his new beliefs, she stopped communicating with him for a long while.

After a rushed trip to Scotland, and with the help of new friends, Cohn considered himself as a messenger of the Messiah. He was reunited with his wife and their children, and returned to New York in 1893. He began a mission in Brownsville, a section of Brooklyn, New York. He experienced many severe episodes of persecution and physical beatings from his people, with whom he valiantly shared his faith until his death on December 19, 1937. He was remembered as a man of a gentle and quiet spirit who wanted his people to know their Messiah. (Rabbi Cohn's story came from a booklet called "Good News," *The Magazine with a Message*, Editor: John During, P.O. Box 7848, Johannesburg, South Africa, Special Rabbis' Edition. Published by Good News Society, 2000., pgs 15-25)

"I went to meetings at this facility twice a week. One meeting was for Bible Study, and the other was for services." Amie told me that her experience at this congregation was very positive.

"It gave me a sense of belonging to a community. The people who went there were smart, as well as engaging. They ranged in age from twenty-something to forty-something, as well as older people. There was always someone to talk to and pray with, regardless of what was going on — whether good or bad. Prayer had a lot of power to change things, and it gave me hope that with faith in God, anything was possible. It helped me have more of a positive outlook, and a new focus because of the time I spent there."

Preparing For College

Mazie encouraged Amie to go to college and make something of herself. She was not sure if she could really accomplish this huge task because of her poor grades in high school, as well as the low scores she received on standardized tests. In any event, she and Mazie made plans to do just that.

Her guidance counselor found a possible college that would accept her since her grade point average was in the low to mid-seventies. It turned out that this college had a special program for students with disabilities. However, before she could be admitted there she had to interview with the Office of Vocational Rehabilitation. She was informed that this agency already had ideas of what would be best for her to pursue in college.

As Amie told me, she really wanted to be a teacher, but the counselor who was assigned to her case disagreed with this idea. She was disabled because she was legally blind, and felt that it was a poor choice.

> "'No one would want a disabled person as their teacher,' she told me. Maybe she was projecting her own experience. Her refusal of my choice really upset me, because that was my dream. If I didn't accept what this counselor wanted me to study, I would not have any backing to pay

for college. So, it was decided that I would study speech therapy. I didn't have a clue what that subject entailed. But maybe there was teaching in there somewhere."

Mazie went with Amie on another interview at the college which qualified her for their program. The chairman of the Department for Students with Disabilities conducted the interview. He explained to Amie that her disability was the reason why her grades were so low, and why she had such difficulty reading and retaining information.

"I was told that I had a visual perceptual learning disability. This meant that I processed reading material slower, which made reading take longer to comprehend. That's why I had such a hard time with it. Focusing on putting letters together to make words was more time consuming. Because that took so much time, comprehending what I read was almost non-existent. I asked him if writing was also part of this, and he said that it was. He explained that writing involved a mental process of eye-hand coordination. This means that a person has to be able to memorize what they see on the blackboard, and be able to copy that information onto paper. Therefore, if I was not able to understand what was written on the blackboard, I would not be able to put that information on paper. That is exactly what happened to me throughout school. The process of writing things out long hand took longer and I would miss half of it before it was all erased. The director told me that there were a few learning

tools available to help me in this task. He sug-
gested using a small tape recorder in class instead
of trying to take notes, and that I needed to let
my professors know that I had permission by
his office to take more time for exams. Finally,
someone understood what I went through and
it all made sense. What a relief! Suddenly, the
thought of going to college was doable."

After her high school graduation, which Mazie attended,
plans were made for Amie to live in the dormitory at the college
she was going to attend. All of her expenses would be covered
between the agency–which gave her a stipend for expenses such
as carfare, books, supplies, and clothing–and the state–which
paid for the tuition, room and board.

"Mazie also gave me some guidelines to keep me
on track as I prepared to go to college. She made
sure that I knew how to handle money by teaching
me how to manage a checkbook. She told me
that part of being on my own was knowing how
to handle money. It was exciting and a bit scary.
How would I handle this new responsibility? I
wasn't going to be able to come back to the res-
idence to talk to Mazie all the time, like I was
used to. Mazie reassured me that she would talk
to me whenever I needed her. She gave me her
home phone number, just in case. That made me
feel better."

"In my high school yearbook she wrote the fol-
lowing to me: 'Dear, Dear Amie, Little One has
grown up–How the time has flown. Life has

much more in store for you. You've learned much — learn also how to have, and enjoy. Continue to grow — to be happy as you are beautiful. Be as strong as the ocean. Love always, Mazie.' What a tribute she gave me! She was always my personal cheerleader. She taught me everything I know. She left no stone unturned. She treated me and all of the girls in the residence as if we were her own children. I don't think that I would have pursued college without her pushing me. I stayed in the group residence over the summer, working to make extra money. In fact, Mazie gave me a going away party so I would have things for the dorm, like sheets, a pillow, a comforter and hangers. Some of the girls chipped in and got me a bathroom caddy for soap and shampoo. It was so thoughtful of her to do something like that! Mazie's gift was a giant alarm clock, in a pretty sea-colored green, so that I would be able to wake up on time for class. It was hard for me to wake up in the morning, and it took a while to get my motor running. Mazie continued to give me her heart, as well as her guidance, for years. There aren't too many people around like that anymore. She was one of a kind."

Many of the girls were not interested in going to college when it was their turn to leave the residence.

"Some of them just wanted to get out on their own. They were tired of the social worker telling them what to do. Most of us didn't realize what was really out there. In a strange way, we were

sheltered from the world, and were only focused on being adjusted to living in the residence. It was a good thing that we had Mazie. She instilled in most of us some of what to expect. Many of the girls though were more interested in working and just being with their boyfriends. We all talked about marriage someday. Mazie told us: 'Education should come before marriage. This way you will be able to provide for yourself and you won't have to be dependent on someone else. Getting to know who you are is part of the process of becoming an adult. Marriage will come, but when you marry it should be at a time when you can be an equal partner.' Mazie wanted all her girls to be independent women. When I left the residence, saying good-bye to Mazie and the other girls was difficult for me. I had made real friends there. I remember that Mazie cried as I was leaving. She gave me a big hug and kiss, as we said good-bye."

The Emergence of Young Adulthood

Amie shared with me that she had a boyfriend during her senior year of high school and wasn't sure how long he would be in the picture after she moved away from the group residence. He wanted to go to pharmacy school, and they would not be able to spend much time together. Eventually, the relationship broke up. Amie was okay with that. She began to focus her time getting accustomed to living in the dorm and doing her studies, which were challenging enough. She met two girls who ended up being her roommates. "I didn't mind that because I was used to it from living in the group residence. We became friends during our first year together." She knew how to do her own laundry, but now she had to pay for it using coin operated machines.

Taking a shower proved to be a different experience. This was due to the fact that the showers were located in the hallway outside of her dorm room.

> "I had to make sure that I had all my stuff and didn't forget anything in the room. I had to carry my towel, toiletries and some of my clothes into the shower room, put it on a bench, and then

bring them back to the room in order to finish getting dressed. Many times the bathroom floors were wet enough for me to slip and fall, so I made sure that I was really careful not to drop anything. In addition, I needed to make sure that my dorm room was locked while at the same time being careful not to lose the key when I went to take a shower. After a while, I made sure that there weren't too many people around so that I could take my time and not be rushed to get out."

This was a co-ed dorm. The boys and girls were on alternating floors. There was an elevator in the building so that Amie did not have to climb the stairs to her floor. The cafeteria was on the ground floor of the building.

"I didn't have a problem with that. You could take what you wanted and go to class. There was a schedule when it was opened, which was pretty flexible. One thing I didn't like was the quiet I heard when the other roommates were not around. I saved up my money and bought a small black and white television and kept it on most of the time, when they weren't in the room, so I wouldn't feel so lonely."

Back then there weren't anywhere near as many channels to watch as there are now, but Amie didn't care. There were other things that Amie began to notice that made her realize that being on her own was more than just a challenge.

"I was thankful that I had a roof over my head, but when my roommates went home for the holidays

or summer vacation, I was allowed to stay in the dorm because I didn't have anywhere else to go. Being alone by myself was so uncomfortable. I missed Mazie most of all, and didn't really have a good relationship with my birth mother at this point. I felt isolated. I called Mazie many times to discuss these things with her. Mazie tried really hard to reassure me that everything was going to be all right, but it didn't always feel that way. I felt that I was missing out on something, being part of a family. I wasn't ready for a family of my own, but I kept hoping that one day it would happen. A few of the girls from the residence did get married after they left the residence, against Mazie's advice, but I couldn't blame them. At least they wouldn't be alone anymore and hopefully make a better life for themselves in the future."

When the next term started, Amie told me that one of my roommates left to live with her boyfriend in the married dorm. She went to say:

"I still had one roommate left and we decided that we didn't want anyone else to be with us. That semester I got a part-time job working in the periodical library in between classes. One of the foster sister's husband had incidentally gone to the same college, and knew the director of the periodical library. I told him who I was in relation to him, and he hired me. My responsibilities were to retrieve the periodicals as requested by students, and then put them back. This job was very convenient, and not too difficult to handle.

It felt good to make extra money. However, the speech pathology major was becoming more difficult. I managed to pass three out of four classes. That fourth class put me over the top. I was not able to do the work for that class because the other work took up most of my time. It caused a big problem for me with the Office of Vocational Rehabilitation, which told me I had to study this in the first place. It was required that I take four classes in order to stay in school. When I explained to the counselor there what I was struggling with, all she could recommend was a tutor. That's all? Didn't she remember what my learning issues were? I guess not. What about all the work it took just to pass these classes? Back then there were no personal computers to work on, or spell check to correct the spelling!"

Amie told me that she had to write papers over and over again on a typewriter, and making foot notes at the bottom of the page just frustrated her beyond measure.

"It seemed to me that there was no working any of this out. I wondered if I could realistically continue with getting my college education. I really didn't like the idea of being a Speech Therapist, and was starting to become disillusioned with the whole process, even though I kept trying. There were a few things that I liked about going to college, such as my job and making new friends who lived in the dorm, and the various activities and events that went on around campus. I enjoyed eating meals with these new friends, and spending

time with them. I learned their ways of studying and how they managed their time. These friends were on a new level. There wasn't any completion between us. They were more helpful."

One of the girls from the congregation, who was a professional pianist, offered to give Amie piano lessons. "I was so excited. I always wanted to learn how to play the piano. She taught me how to read music and play the piano. I remember hearing a story that a physical therapist told the Italian foster family, way back when, that learning piano would be beneficial in order to help my fingers develop, but of course that never happened. So when she offered to do this with me, I took her up on it. My school had a piano room that was available to students free of charge. We had such fun together. It was only for a short time, because she met a guy at the congregation, got married, and moved away soon after that. This experience will always be a fond memory for me."

An Early Marriage

These new friends were becoming a real support for Amie.

"I was getting a bit more comfortable in my own skin. Some of my friends at the congregation were making marriage plans, while a few of the girls from the residence were doing the same thing. Mazie was still there, helping me stay focused. I thought about what it would be like to be married, but who would want to take me on with my disability? Would there be anyone out there that I could really trust? I had no one to answer to, and any decision like that was up to me."

Jane was already married, and was struggling. I knew how much Jane wanted her marriage to work. I didn't want that to happen. Yet the idea of being alone didn't feel right. Nor did becoming sexually active without a commitment for the future seem good, either. I didn't want to end up like my birth mother. I decided to wait until I met someone with similar values, hoping it wouldn't take too long. I continued to attend the congregation and participate in its various activities.

In the fall of my second year of college, I met a handsome young man named Alex who was in his first year of law school. The leader of the congregation introduced me to him before the weekly Tuesday night Bible study. He asked me to come along and eat dinner with them. The restaurant was down the block from the congregation. In this restaurant, you ordered your food by a menu on a big billboard, went to a table and then a server would come out and bring you what you ordered. Anyway, we sat down at a table, and both men started talking. Occasionally I would say something, but for the most part I just watched and listened to their conversation. I noticed that Alex was very engaging. He liked to talk and asked me questions about myself when we left the restaurant. I couldn't take my eyes off his pretty blue eyes. He seemed to be very sincere. After a few weeks, Alex asked me out on a date. I didn't expect that. We went to another local restaurant near the congregation before the Bible study. He made a comment to me about my eating. I ordered a salad because I was always on a diet until I saw ice cream or chocolate chip cookies! Anyway, he said, 'I am glad to see that you enjoy your food.' I wasn't sure how to take that comment but he went on to explain that some of the girls he dated just picked at their food and didn't finish it. He liked that I enjoyed eating. I liked spending time with Alex and thought he would be a good friend. I didn't bring any hopes into this relationship, because I didn't want to get hurt, or hurt him."

To Amie's surprise, he really seemed interested in her, and was not negatively affected by her disability. He came across as a very kind person.

> "He even visited me in the dorm and gave me a present for my birthday. It was a hat with a matching scarf. How thoughtful and sweet of him. About a month later, after Bible study, he wanted to talk and had to catch a train to go home to a suburb outside the city. He asked me to walk as far as I could with him. The station was a couple of miles away. I held on to his arm as we walked. I remember that he talked a lot and asked me lots of questions. I got pretty close to the train station he needed. It surprised me that I walked all that distance. I got on the subway and went back to the dorm. He called me the next day and told me that he had a good time with me and that he wanted to see me again next week."

Their second date was also very memorable. They went to dinner at a famous cheesecake restaurant across the street from the college Amie attended. Amie laughed as she told me about what happened during this date. "I ordered a salad and Alex ate most of it." She thought it was strange, but didn't say anything about it to him, not to embarrass him. "I was just happy that he wanted to spend time with me."

As time progressed, Amie noticed that Alex wanted to spend more time with her, and he would re-arrange his classes so that he could do just that.

> "He called me frequently, and we spent a lot of time just talking about life and faith. Alex was

very knowledgeable about the Bible and we believed and agreed on many of the same things. Alex was also a hard worker. He went to classes, as well as having a part-time job, just like I did. He was a better student and got B+'s and A's against my B's and C's."

Sometime later, Alex gave Amie a piece of jewelry. It was a small, shimmering Jewish star on a fourteen-carat gold chain. "It was very pretty, and I was proud to wear it." Amie said that she was still very self-conscious about her appearance. "I was a bit chubby at the time, and wondered if that bothered Alex. I wasn't really ready to diet again. Besides, most of our time together was spent eating in a restaurant, and he never mentioned it."

Alex confided in Amie that he really was falling in love with her and wanted to marry her. This was just short of four months after they started dating.

> "I thought that was nice, but wasn't sure if I was marriage material. The truth was that I really liked him, but didn't understand what being in love was all about, and didn't want to hurt him. I felt that it might be wrong to marry someone who I wasn't in love with."

Amie shared with me that most of what she understood about the concept of being in love was what she saw in the movies.

> "Yet I couldn't resist the idea of having someone in my life who was willing to take care of me. That was always in the back of my mind. There really

hadn't been anyone whom she felt really loved by, except Mazie, but that was more of a motherly love. She wondered if she was even worthy of such a love. Alex told me that he had enough love for both of us. That was so sweet of him to say. 'Could anyone really feel that way?' I wondered. I really had to think about this. Alex was also very convincing. I wanted to make sure that he wasn't just attracted to me and didn't feel sorry for me. I finally said yes."

It was an answer to her prayers, because Amie told me that she wanted to marry someone who believed in Jesus like she did, and who came from a Jewish background.

After Amie said yes, it was time to go and pick out a ring. "We went to the diamond district in the city and Alex picked out a pretty, old fashioned looking one in yellow gold. The stone was small, but I was happy with it." Amie told me that she wanted to show it to Mazie, and to Kellie. "I went to visit her at the residence, and she was very happy for me." She offered to have her wedding reception at the residence. Mazie felt that it was important for Amie to be proud of what she had accomplished and show off a bit. Kellie was also happy and wanted to be invited to their wedding. "I told her that she would definitely be invited, and I would let her know when we picked a date for the wedding."

The next step was for Alex to tell his family the news. At that time, his family was not so thrilled about their son's choice for a wife. The reason for that was because they felt that Amie came from "the wrong side of the tracks" and had a handicap. They really did not understand who Amie was, or think that she had anything to offer their son. Amie had no family or any money to speak of; she did not come from their class of people.

"I was hurt at first, but I couldn't blame them. On the surface they didn't know what to expect. When Alex brought me to their home, they had a house just like all the foster families did. It was decorated nicely, and there was a grand piano in the living room. I didn't say much, just watched and listened to Alex talk to his parents as he tried to explain why he wanted to marry me. We knew that they weren't very happy, and it would take time for them to accept things. Alex decided that he wanted to get married during the winter intercession before the spring semester."

This way both Alex and Amie would have at least one month for the wedding, the honeymoon, and the setting up of their apartment before the next semester began.

There was a lot of excitement going on. "Mazie and I worked on the guest list, as well as the food." Mazie asked one of the girls who lived in the residence before Amie if she would be willing to make a bouquet of flowers for Amie for the reception. "She said yes and they turned out so beautiful it made me cry. Mazie even made time to go to a store and pick out a wedding dress."

Amie told me this was something moms do with their daughters.

"I was so touched that she offered. The first place we went to had a dress that interested me. You could call it a peasant style dress. It was off-white, had a square neck line and was embroidered with flowers that were the same color as the dress. The material was a stretched knit, and the bridal

manager put a bridal slip underneath the dress to make it look like a wedding dress. It looked beautiful!"

Amie says that dress still hangs in her closet just to remind her of that wonderful day.

Alex's family, especially his mother, was still upset about this wedding. The reason was that she wanted Alex to be married in the Jewish tradition. Alex and Amie's belief in Jesus was considered a conversion to Christianity, so her rabbi would not marry them. Alex's mother finally found a Jewish judge to perform the ceremony. "That must have been a huge compromise for her, and she seemed to feel better. Later on one of Alex's relatives told me that she had a talk with his parents, expressed to them that she didn't feel that I would take Alex away from them, but rather wanted to be part of his family." Amie saw that Alex was different from his family, and maybe that was more disturbing for them than just her.

Just one month before the wedding, Alex got very sick. He went home to the doctor with symptoms of a high fever, achiness and a very sore throat. The doctor informed him that he had contracted mononucleosis. This was considered highly contagious. That meant that Amie was not able to see Alex much. He was home for more than three weeks.

"I was so worried that Alex wouldn't be better in time for the wedding. Would he be strong enough? He also had to take his finals. His mother had to drive him to school, wait for him to take the final and drive him back home again for three days. Alex told me that he didn't think that he was able to pass them because he was feeling weak and couldn't concentrate. When he

was done, he slept in the car on the way back. The extreme fatigue and need for sleep was part of this sickness, and the doctor told him that it would take a few months for him to get back to his full strength, and to take it easy."

When the wedding took place, Alex was no longer contagious. Alex thought it would be a good idea to go to the honeymoon haven in a nearby state for their honeymoon. He heard that the food was good. Besides, this particular place was not that expensive. It was only a two hour drive away, and Alex liked to drive.

Alex and Amie had their wedding ceremony on a Friday and had their reception on Sunday at the group residence. Many members of Alex's family attended, as well as Amie's Italian foster family. Mazie thought it was important that her birth mother and half-sister should be there.

> "I wasn't too comfortable with that, but my birth mother was happy to be invited. During the reception, the foster mother had a talk with Mazie to thank her for looking after me. I didn't remember eating very much of anything. Most of the time was given to answering the family questions about who I was, and how me and Alex had met. Mazie did a wonderful job hosting this for us."

When the reception was over, Amie and Alex went to their three room apartment to get ready for their honeymoon. This apartment was part of a three family house. The apartment was located in the back of the house. The kitchen was old, but the stove and refrigerator worked. The living room was really small. It fit a small couch and chair. A friend helped Amie re-cover an

old fashioned recliner. There was barely enough room to put a desk in there for Alex to study. The bedroom was big enough for a double bed, two end tables and two dressers. The house took in lots of sun, so it didn't seem that small. It was also on the ground floor.

> "While we were on our honeymoon, Alex's parents came to our apartment to bring the wedding gifts. People were so generous to us. Little did they know that the next day we would have to drive through a snowstorm. We were able to stay for a week in a cabin. The food was good, but Alex was so tired after the day's activities that he slept really soundly. I wondered how long it would take for him to recover.
> He was really comfortable with things. It wasn't as easy for me. Things that would be considered to be a natural occurrence took more time. I didn't like being alone if Alex wasn't nearby. At the residence and the dorm at college, there were always people around and I didn't feel alone. We bought a television for the living room and I left it on most of the time so I could hear people talking."

Alex was happy that Amie was finally living with him. One of the biggest adjustments Amie had was sharing the bed with Alex. Amie told me that she never slept with someone before and was not sexually active before the wedding. Neither was Alex. Amie said that she was a little embarrassed to share this, but felt that it was important to be honest. This was really new to both of them. "We both decided to wait until marriage to have sex. I shared with Alex that I didn't want to be like my birth mother and he agreed to wait."

Amie had to learn how to cook and keep house. Alex helped her with the housework, but was not good at cooking. Amie remembers that, "I made many calls to Mazie about how to cook and what to cook." As she learned these skills, Amie told me that "what we ate got better. Alex liked almost anything. I did learn to cook and he always complimented me for cooking for him."

Amie felt that Alex was someone who taught her what real love was about. He was very kind and very loving towards her. "He has always been able to love me and our friends more unconditionally than I was. Alex has found it easy to put others first, as well as being able to take in the other person's point of view and their welfare, even if he disagreed with that person."

At first Amie would be upset about it when it came to doing this with other people. She thought that Alex was taking their side. She really could not understand this, but now thinks of it as a gift. Alex had an ability to put his feelings aside for the most part, even if it came to spiritual things. He told Amie many times, "It isn't our job to change people's minds. That is up to God, and all we can do is pray for them."

As Amie and Alex became adjusted to each other, they also had to figure out about paying their own bills.

> "Each of us held down-part time jobs, while taking a full load of classes in college and law school. After classes, Alex went to work for a local law firm. To make extra money, Alex would drive a cab in the town he grew up in on the week end. He even got his father a job driving the cab in his retirement."

Amie and Alex would stay over at his parents' house in order to do this until he graduated from law school. Amie continued

to work in the college periodicals library after classes until she changed schools.

Within a year or so, things started to become overwhelming for Amie. She was having trouble keeping up the pace of going to classes, working, studying and having enough time to spend with Alex. Both of their schedules were hectic, and money was really tight. She began to realize that they both had a different value system when it came to handling money.

> "I was both a spender as well as a saver. Alex was a giver. However, I thought that Alex was supposed to take care of things. I gave him my paycheck, and when I asked him for something, he would always come back to me with, 'Why do you need that? What's it for?' I would try to explain what I wanted, but if he felt that it wasn't necessary, he would say no. We argued a lot over money and how to spend it. It was his feeling that if I made do without it, someone else could use it. After a while, I just wouldn't ask for anything I knew that Alex would say no to. It reminded me of the foster homes, and I just couldn't make Alex understand that I felt deprived. It was hard on me. I didn't handle my money like that before. I didn't spend much because I didn't have much. I felt if you needed something, you should have it. I would save up for something if I didn't have the money right away. Alex misunderstood my needs. He never had to save up for anything. If he needed something, his parents would buy it for him."

Amie told me that sometimes Alex would give people money without telling her because he didn't like arguing with

her about it. Alex enjoyed giving Amie gifts for her birthday. When it came to holidays like Christmas, Chanukah or Easter, Alex didn't believe in giving gifts for them. His parents gave him money most of the time for any gift. That wasn't as important to him as it was for Amie.

"I still missed Christmas and Easter, but especially Christmas. I wanted to celebrate them with Alex, but he wasn't familiar with them and didn't want to. He only wanted to celebrate Chanukah and Passover, which were unfamiliar to me. For my first Chanukah with him, he bought me a little bear. We celebrated Passover with his family. The important thing was that Alex liked spending time with me. He enjoyed taking me places that were free of charge or very low cost. I went anywhere Alex wanted to go. The best times we had were in his car. We talked most of the time, and he tried to help me understand his points of view, and make me not worry so much. He was always able to back his point up with a Scripture verse. I couldn't argue with that. Alex had the right to his opinion, and I to mine. But I thought that we should agree on things, more often than not. We were supposed to have differences, and that was okay. But it didn't feel right to think that way. I didn't really understand how Alex could be different from me in his thinking. We didn't have to agree on everything. Yet there was a part of me that wanted us to think the same on everything. I thought that way we were really one unit. I didn't realize that we were supposed to be separate but equal partners."

Alex was of the opinion that being married should have helped Amie feel better about herself.

> "It did sometimes, but sometimes it didn't. There were more responsibilities with living with someone with all the give and take. I realized that if something happened to upset me, I was only able to look at it negatively, while Alex saw things positively. He was the optimist and I was the perpetual pessimist. That was probably due to the fact that I tended to worry more than he did."

It came to a head within three years. Amie started experiencing anxiety attacks. She said that this really frightened her. The panic attacks made her worry that she was going to die. "I went to the doctor, and he prescribed tranquilizers. The only problem was that they didn't work. My legs felt really heavy to walk with and I was really tired all the time, and my fearful thinking didn't go away. Traveling became more cumbersome."

Amie told me of a real scary incident that occurred while she was traveling to school on the train by herself, which reinforced her anxieties.

> "There were two men who came on the subway train. They began to stare at me menacingly. I thought that they were going to follow me after I got off the train. I tried to look around and see if they were really following me after I went up the stairs in the station. By that point I was crying, and made my way to a phone booth to call Alex. As I was trying to tell him what happened, still crying, a police officer came up to me and asked if I was a runaway. I told the officer that I was

calling my husband for help, but he didn't believe me. I think that was because I was crying so hard, and had a young face. I was only twenty-three at the time. He asked me to come into the office. I told him what happened on the train, and then he asked me for Alex's phone number at work to make sure that I was telling the truth. When he talked to Alex, he realized that I was telling the truth, and he apologized and suggested that Alex come and pick me up, because I was so upset. He gave me the phone and I told Alex where I was and waited for him to come get me. After that incident I didn't want to take the subway to school any more. We worked out a way for Alex to drop me off at school and then pick me up after I was done. His job gave him the flexibility to do that for me, and I was so thankful. This happened during my final semester of school for the two year degree."

By the time the semester was over, Amie found out that she was pregnant with their first child.

Raising Her First Child Without a Mother

Now with an Associate's Degree in Early Childhood Education in hand, Amie was excited that she and Alex could now focus on the baby that was to come into their lives. As the pregnancy progressed she was getting very anxious about her ability to be a mother.

> "I didn't know what to expect. I was never pregnant before. Mazie was the first person I called when I found out the news. She was really happy for me. Then I called Jane. By that point she had delivered her first child, a beautiful, healthy girl. If I wasn't on the phone with Mazie, I was on the phone with Jane. We talked a lot and she encouraged and shared with me her experience, which was very positive. I was still experiencing panic attacks. I thought it might be helpful to see a counselor to help lower them, as well as get through the pregnancy. I found a believing psychologist in the city, but to my dismay he wasn't on the same page with me. He felt that I should have an abortion because of the anxiety attacks,

and thought I really wasn't ready for a child. I was so surprised by his reaction. I couldn't bail out now. I didn't know how I would do it, but his comments gave me the determination to go forward with the pregnancy and be a good mother. I told the counselor, 'Thank you for your time,' and walked out."

Money was still tight, but Alex now had a new, more permanent job as a legal researcher for an appeals court. Amie had done some part-time jobs, but was unable to keep them due to lack of experience. She tried really hard, but had trouble with some of her bosses. They teased her for fun, like the other co-workers, but Amie couldn't handle it.

"By the time I was three months pregnant, I found a doctor who was on our insurance, who was willing to take care of the delivery of the baby. I asked him if our baby would have any disabilities because of me and he reassured me that it wasn't hereditary. He said with proper prenatal care, I would be fine, and so would the baby. That was so good to hear, and my anxiety level went down a few pegs."

The summer was approaching and she began to experience what it was like being pregnant.

"By this time, I was five months pregnant and the baby was very busy moving inside of me. Some of my girlfriends at their congregation were also pregnant and were having their first child too. We became our own support group. As my body

began to change with a growing belly, I needed more physical help. The first thing I did was buy a support pregnancy girdle to help carry the extra weight of the pregnancy. It was designed to support the lower abdomen by lifting it above the pelvis for balance. I also had to get a cane to walk so I wouldn't fall. I needed some maternity clothes. A few ladies gave me maternity tops. I only had to buy maternity pants. Alex and I went looking for a crib and dresser for the baby. We found one on sale and we didn't have to pay for it until after the baby was born."

"One of my friends from the congregation hosted a baby shower for me. That was so kind of her. It was fun opening presents for the baby. I felt so loved by these ladies. They too were excited for me, and prayed that the baby would be healthy and that I would have a good delivery."

As Amie came closer to her due date, she was starting to get nervous. One of her friends from the Italian foster home just happened to call her and told her of her new baby boy.

"She told me that she had to have a C-section in order to deliver him. I wondered if that was going to happen to me. A few other women I knew went through the same thing. 'Was this a sign?' I thought to myself. Should I prepare for this, too? I asked the doctor about it, and he couldn't give me any guarantee, since my pelvis was small, and it would depend on how the labor was doing. There was no way to know in advance."

Alex tried really hard to help Amie through this. He was excited that they were going to be parents. He was also a bit nervous, and wondered what fatherhood would be like for him. He told Amie that he always respected his father growing up, and wanted to be like his father.

In preparation for the birth of the baby, Amie and Alex went to Lamaze classes. Here, they learned about the process of labor and delivery. The premise of the Lamaze method is controlling the pain in labor through breathing. These classes provided lots of information so that there wouldn't be any surprises.

> "Since an ultrasound was not available, Alex and I wondered what the sex of the baby was going to be. We picked out names for a boy and a girl. If the baby was a girl, the name was going to be Elisabeth. It means, 'devoted one.' If the baby was a boy, the name was going to be Samuel. It means, 'God heard.'"

Interestingly enough, most of the other couples who were having babies had boys. Amie shared with me that Alex wanted a boy, and she wanted a girl. The due date was supposed to be Christmas Day. "I had hoped that the baby would not be born on that holiday. Alex's mother was born on Christmas. I wanted the baby to have his own day. The baby was born six days early. Labor started early in the morning. It was really painful. It was like having a bad menstrual cycle."

Amie knew that she had to go to get ready for the hospital. "I took a shower and cried that this day finally arrived. After I got dressed, Alex drove me to the hospital and we met the doctor there." The labor pains were getting more intense and were physically more difficult to tolerate. Those breathing techniques went right out the window. "Forget that! I wanted it to

stop and have this baby already." The doctor had the anesthesiologist administer medication by IV to speed up her labor, but it back-fired. "My legs started to spasm, and I didn't have any control over them. They would bend and cramp up to my chest. Alex didn't know what to do. He was getting tired also, trying to help me breathe. The spasms interfered with the breathing, so he just sat down in a chair next to me and held my hand."

> After seeing what was happening to Amie, the doctor decided that it would be safer for her to have to have a C-section after all. "It was the only way I could have this baby. He examined me and said that the baby's head was big, and wasn't sure that he would get through the birth canal without a problem. I was so disappointed that I couldn't get through the labor."

After thirteen hours of labor, Amie was wheeled into the operating room. Alex was not allowed to be in the room with her.

> "Then I got really scared. The doctor gave me the option of having a spinal, or to be put to sleep to have the baby. I decided to be put to sleep because I was afraid that something would happen to my back. Before the anesthesia was given to me I prayed, 'Please God, don't let me die, and keep my baby safe.'" Within an hour, Amie's baby was born. It was a boy! He weighed eight pounds and four ounces. He was born around 3:20 that afternoon. "I had to be woken up to be told. Thank God everything was all right. I got to see him. He looked perfect. He had real flushed cheeks, and a head full of dark brown hair. As soon as the

nurse showed him to me, I fell back to sleep on and off the rest of the day. I didn't get to see him again until 9:30 at night. I knew that he was my baby because we had the same name tags on our wrists. He was so perfectly normal. He had all his fingers and toes, and when he opened his eyes, they were blue just like his daddy. He was named after one of his grandfathers in keeping with his family tradition. Alex and I were so thrilled that everything turned out great. Alex said, 'I have a happy mother, with a healthy baby. What more could you ask for?'"

"The next day I was in a lot of pain, due to the afterbirth contractions and the C-section incision. The doctor gave me pain medication and it helped me have enough strength to stay awake and spend the day with Samuel for each feeding. I decided beforehand that I wanted to nurse him, and was determined to make this birth experience a success. Samuel was a hungry baby, and a good 'nurser.' I was given a walker to use to get to the bathroom and to lean on as I took a shower. The nurse on duty would watch the baby for me while I was in the shower, and then when I got back to the chair or bed, help me get settled to nurse him. By that point he was really crying and hungry. Each time he entered the room our ID bracelets had to match. This was part of the hospital security procedure."

Alex's family and their friends came to see Samuel. Due to the fact that Amie had a C-section, she was allowed to stay at

the hospital for eight days. The day before she and Samuel left the hospital, he was circumcised.

"When Alex and I brought Samuel home from the hospital, I cried as we walked into our apartment.

I was so nervous."

Alex's mother offered to pay for a baby nurse for a week, so that Amie could get back her strength.

> "That was very kind of her. The baby nurse changed and bathed Samuel, and washed his clothes. Friends came over with cooked meals for us. Alex went back to work a few days later. I was able to get around on my own without the walker, but I held onto walls instead. Within a few months I was doing really well. When we went outside to go food shopping or to a congregation meeting, Alex held the baby for me in a baby carrier. I was able to use a stroller for the baby when I was by myself. I also got in touch with a support group for nursing mothers called La Leche League. The meeting place was at another nursing mother's house once a month. We talked about how to nurse successfully, and basic parenting. I found it very helpful and it made me feel that I was doing something right."

Amie told me that she even used a diaper service for Samuel because she felt cloth diapers were better for his skin than disposables. Not many people used diaper services back then. Disposable diapers had come into being and they were considered more convenient.

When Samuel was three months old, the congregation they were attending had a baby dedication service. One of the leaders

from the Beth Sar Shalom fellowship came to officiate it. He quoted the Scripture about the story of Hannah, who prayed to the Lord for a child (see I Samuel Chapter 1). Amie and Alex were so proud of Samuel. "We hosted a little party afterwards at our apartment. My friend who gave me the baby shower helped decorate and prepare food for the party. It was such a joy to celebrate having Samuel in our lives."

Samuel was a very good baby Amie told me. As he began to grow and move around, Amie felt that she was going to need help taking care of him physically. By chance, she met a nice young girl in their local park and began to stir up a conversation. Irene was married and had a little girl of her own named Shauna.

"We would meet almost every weekday in the early afternoon, after our babies had their first nap of the day. While we swung our babies on the baby swings, we would talk about what our babies were doing, and compare notes. Within a month of our meeting, we thought it would be a good idea to meet each other's spouses. Irene's husband Noel, just happened to be an accountant. Most of our time was spent in the local park with our babies. On occasion, we would go shopping together at the local supermarket and nearby department store if we needed to buy something for the babies. Irene and I were a good tag team. She was very helpful to me in carrying Samuel as he got bigger and moved around more. Her daughter was not as active as Samuel, so I was able to help Irene take care of her. They also liked each other and played together. We would plan dinners after our husbands came home from work

after a long afternoon in the park. It wasn't long after that all of us became close friends. Irene and I invited each other to family parties, and everyone thought that we were related.

By the time Samuel reached nine months old, Amie felt that she needed even more help emotionally. Samuel was thriving, and sometimes it seemed to Amie that she did not know how to handle some of the things that Samuel did. She started to have trouble coping, and began to get overwhelmed.

At that time she was taking piano lessons from a person whose son was seeing a therapist. He thought this person was really effective and helpful with his son, and highly recommended her.

> "I decided that I would meet with [the therapist] and see if she would be able to help. At our first meeting, I felt very comfortable with her. She told me that she could help me with learning parenting skills to raise Samuel, as well as help me work through leftover issues of being in foster care. Her name was Luisa. It was very insightful to learn what to expect from Samuel, and to help me set limits with him."

This issue was difficult for Amie because she wanted Samuel to be happy, and setting limits only reminded her of being punished. Amie told me that she did not want to hurt him in any way, and she thought that setting limits would hurt him. She also thought that saying *no* would mean that he would not love her anymore. But the 'D' word of discipline had to be consistent.

Luisa taught Amie that setting boundaries would help Samuel with self-control in the long run. She also explored with

Amie to define her role as Samuel's mother, as well as Alex's wife. In this process Amie learned several important things, including how to teach Samuel to get along with others, and not just think about his own needs.

> "There were three main things that Luisa taught me. The first was that one should never give another person control over their own emotions. Emotional control has to come from the inside, not the outside. Second, when you have a relationship with another person, what one gives out does not always guarantee that the other person will reciprocate in kind. She said, 'The contract does not always work both ways.' Third, one should never make promises. If one makes a promise, it is expected to be kept no matter what, especially when it comes to children. It is a good practice with adults also, because many times people's feelings get hurt and that could cause a rift between them. It is better to be able to give something to someone without expecting anything in return. This goes along with the scripture verse where Jesus said: 'And just as you want men to do to you, you also do to them likewise,' (see Luke 6:31)."

Luisa gave Amie a gift. She helped Amie cultivate and incorporate the knowledge necessary to help her mother her son, in spite of the fact that Amie never had a mother of her own. It was a slow growth process, but Amie allowed herself to experience past pains, and used them to work through the challenges she faced. She shared, "It has been said that parents are to be the

teachers of children, but the truth is that one's children are the real teachers of their parents."

Amie shared with me that Samuel was a normal, active baby. He was a good eater and enjoyed playing with other children. He learned how to do things quickly, and was walking by the time he was a year old. He also began to talk at an early age. This made it easier for Amie to handle his needs, because she did not have to carry him.

> "I did more of taking care of Samuel's physical needs, like bathing, feeding, and changing his diapers. I didn't take my eyes off of him. The housework went by the wayside, except for cooking meals and laundry. I would read to him when there was a quiet moment, show him how to play with his toys, and watch *Sesame Street* with him. I also taught him how to go up and down the stairs by himself. This is how I did it: I would stand behind him and physically put each leg on the step until he learned how to do this himself. Going down was a bit more challenging. At first I would sit him on my lap and move my bottom down each step one at a time until we reached the last step. Then he was able to go where he wanted. Eventually, I taught him to slide down on his belly. He laughed and enjoyed doing that. I was always right there so he wouldn't get hurt. Samuel enjoyed washing dishes with me by standing on a child step stool. Both of us got wet. Doing the dishes with Samuel reminded me of the time Mazie spent with me as I did the dishes at the residence. If I was outside of the apartment with Alex and Samuel, I relied on Alex to carry

him or run after him whenever he tried to get away. Samuel was a very busy baby, and he kept us going."

When Samuel turned one year old, Amie and Alex had a big party for him. "We invited Alex's family and some close friends, including Irene, Noel and Shauna. Alex liked making birthday celebrations." Amie was glad that he made such a fuss. "This was one of our first traditions we created together going forward. Alex would say, 'Happy Birthday week.'"

Alex and Amie decided that she would stay home and raise Samuel. By the time he reached a year old, "I thought it would be a good idea to go back to college on a part-time basis so that if I ever needed to work outside the home, I would eventually have the degree and have some useful skills to do so." There was a local college where she could resume her studies one class at a time; that way it wouldn't interfere with caring for Samuel. Her goal was to obtain a four year degree. Amie felt comfortable majoring in Humanities and Education. This, of course, would take years, but Amie was not in a hurry.

ANOTHER CHILD ON THE WAY

By the time Samuel was two years old, Amie and Alex were talking about having another baby. They thought it would be good for Samuel to have a sibling by the time he was three years old.

It turned out that Amie and Alex had their second child when Samuel was three years, and four months old. This baby came in the spring time, and the week before he was born it was very hot.

Amie went into labor on the expected due date. "We had to leave Samuel with Irene and Noel, so that Alex and I could go to the hospital to deliver the baby."

When Amie and Alex arrived at the hospital, Amie was experiencing good labor.

> "The doctor examined me, and I was told that I would have to have another C-section. I was so disappointed and overheard a nurse comment that I would never be able to deliver that baby because he was too big. It took a little convincing by the doctor that I had to deliver this way, but I could have an epidural and be awake for the birth of this child. That option made it seem a little better."

Amie was concerned that the injection would not work, but it did and the baby was born. It was another boy! He was bigger than Samuel and weighed eight pounds, fourteen ounces. Amie remembers that when she saw how big he was, she felt better that the doctor decided to deliver the baby by Cesarean section. "He looked different than Samuel. He had light brown hair, and had really big shoulders." He was named after another one of Alex's grandfathers. "We named him Benjamin. It means, 'Son of the right hand.'"

As Amie did with Samuel, she was able to stay in the hospital for eight days. Benjamin was also circumcised the day before Amie left with him to go home. Amie's friend Irene said that Samuel was a sad little boy without his mother. Alex brought Samuel to see Amie and his new little brother. He was glad to see his mother, but not sure about his brother. It would take Samuel time to adjust to Benjamin.

Amie's hands were full, and so was her heart. "I didn't experience any postpartum depression. I was so thrilled that I had delivered another healthy baby. All I wanted was that my boys were strong and happy little guys."

Just like they did with Samuel, Amie and Alex had a baby dedication for baby Benjamin.

"Benjamin was truly another gift from God. He was such a sweet baby. He didn't cry very much. I was a little more comfortable taking care of him, by this time I had my friend Irene come and help with carrying Benjamin until I was able. It took about two weeks until I could carry Benjamin on my own. I didn't need a baby nurse. Irene helped me make meals, and her daughter and Samuel would play together. As much as possible, I encouraged Samuel's involvement in the

care of Benjamin. I decided to have Samuel and Benjamin in bed with me so that Samuel could get used to him and bond with him. I was able to nurse Benjamin, and Samuel helped with getting diapers and talking to him when he cried. I needed to create a system to handle both boys. I tried to keep them close to me in one room at a time. I followed Samuel wherever he went around the house, and took Benjamin with me. I used the high chair, the play pen and stroller a lot to keep Benjamin safe, so that I wouldn't fall with him. Going outside was more of a challenge. First, I had to put the double stroller outside, then place Benjamin in the front part of the stroller, and then make sure that Samuel sat in the back part of the stroller. The only place I was comfortable with was going to the park down the block. This way Samuel could run around, swing on the swing, and get some of his energy out as well as get fresh air. That was good for all of us. Sometimes I took them to the local supermarket to get perishables like milk, bread and eggs. We went to the local butcher, fruit and vegetable store to buy these items daily, so that they would be fresh. This helped us as a family to eat healthy, and it was good for me to walk to the stores for exercise."

Amie made sure that she did not stay in these stores too long, because Samuel would want to get out of the stroller before she was done. If Samuel got out of the stroller he would run ahead of her, and Amie wasn't sure she could catch up to him on her own. "When we got home from shopping I was so

relieved. Most of the time it was easier to stay home with the boys in the house, until Irene came over or Alex came home."

Benjamin was truly a happy baby. He always smiled. He only cried when he was hungry. Like Samuel, he walked and began talking by the time he was a year old. He also was a very busy baby. Amie said that one needed to have eyes behind one's head to keep up with him!

Amie cultivated her hearing skills, and never went anywhere without someone to help find Benjamin. He had a tendency to walk off so that he could go look at something. Benjamin was a quick learner because he had Samuel to teach him, Amie told me.

> "By this time, my friend Irene had her second child. We then were able to help each other even more. We spent most of the weekdays together, creating our own day care center."

Amie went back to college again when Benjamin was a year old. Samuel also started pre-school a few days a week.

> "He didn't really like it at first when Amie dropped him off. He cried, 'Mommy, don't leave me here.' I cried too, but I reassured him that I would come back for him soon, and eventually he liked it. Benjamin liked when Samuel was around and was happy when it was time to pick his brother up. I would put Benjamin in the stroller and walk to Samuel's pre-school, and then we would walk back home again."

Both of these boys were a real handful. They were very active little boys. Amie told me that one time Benjamin followed their friends out the front door, and almost found himself in front

of the garbage truck in the street in front of their house. Amie was able to stop him just in time from getting too close to the truck and bring him safely back into the house.

Another time, Amie had to interview someone for a class she was taking. Alex had brought Benjamin into this person's apartment, which was on the fifth floor, and caught him just before he fell out of a window that had been left wide open. It was definitely a scary moment. "It still scares Alex and me when we think about it," Amie told me.

Alex liked to take the family on outings where the boys would have physical activities to participate in. Some of the places included Six Flags theme park, and road trips to explore famous sites. They both participated in day camps to learn how to swim. Amie thought it was important to have that survival skill.

Finally, a "Daughter Girl"

When Benjamin reached three years old, Alex and Amie talked about having one more child. Amie wanted a girl. It didn't matter to Alex, yet he felt it was better to wait until Benjamin was a little older because he was so busy. Amie agreed and she got pregnant when Benjamin was four years old, and was in pre-school. This baby was due in the late spring, and to Amie's surprise it was going to be a girl. Amie was so excited that she "bought out the store" with little girl things.

This time around, Amie knew that she was going to have a C-section. She was not surprised. She just wanted to have a healthy baby. During this pregnancy, both boys came down with the chicken pox. Amie had chicken pox when she was a young girl, so the baby was not in danger. It was hard on the boys.

Benjamin got a worse case of it than Samuel. Amie helped the boys feel better with warm baths and calamine lotion. Irene's children also contracted it, so they had someone to play with. Within a month or so, the boys and Irene's children were back to normal, running around like "chickens without a head." Alex's mother used to say that Alex got it back in spades because he was just like them. But Alex didn't think so; he just thought they were active boys.

This baby was going to be named after one of Alex's grandmothers. "When she was born, we decided to name her

Elisabeth, which means, 'Devoted one.' I gave birth to this baby in the late afternoon, and the boys went to Irene's house after school. Benjamin kept saying that 'my mommy is having a baby.'"

After the baby was born, Alex ran out of the recovery room to call everyone about Elisabeth. He was so excited! He loved Amie so much, and now he had a little girl to love. She was the smallest in weight. She weighed seven pounds and ten ounces. Alex and the boys came to see Amie and the baby that evening. Like with the other babies, she was allowed to stay eight days.

"Elisabeth was so good at nursing that the milk went up through her nose! She was also a very sweet baby. She looked more delicate and seemed to be so tiny compared to the boys. I was a little nervous about caring for her. I asked another friend, Rochelle, who had two girls, to come over and show me how to bathe Elisabeth. She told me not to be so nervous, and showed me how to do it. After a while I got the hang of it and Elisabeth grew and developed just like her brothers.
I wanted to send out a girly birth announcement. Rochelle helped me design one. She drew a long vintage dress on the cover of the announcement, which was on pink paper, of course. On the inside it said that a baby girl was added to Amie and Alex's household."

The boys were very happy that their mommy had a little girl. They were so excited when she got home. Amie told me that Benjamin liked to wake her up and carry her to Amie when she cried. "I think that Benjamin liked her so much because he wanted her attention. He was such a strong little boy. He

didn't seem jealous of her. Both Samuel and Benjamin really liked Elisabeth, and enjoyed caring for her."

When Elisabeth was four months old she, like her brothers, was dedicated to the Lord at a special service in our home. Luisa gave Amie Elisabeth's first real dress as a gift, and she put it on Elisabeth for that service. "She looked so pretty. I even had pictures of her taken in that dress."

Just like her brothers had, Elisabeth walked and started talking around a year old. She was a picky eater, and was more fussy about food.

Something strange happened to Amie when Elisabeth turned two years old. "Zelda tried to contact me and let me know that she was in the hospital facing cancer." This really frightened Amie. She wondered what her birth mother wanted from her.

Amie had severed ties with her birth mother after she had given birth to Samuel because she did not want him to know about his grandmother's drug addiction. She was trying to protect him from that. She wanted Samuel to have a normal childhood.

As it turned out, Amie's birth mother and half-sister were both in the hospital together. There was no one to care for her sister at home, so they put admitted her with her birth-mother. Alex wanted to visit them, but Amie just could not handle it. A short time later, Amie received a call that her birth mother had passed away, and that the state wanted to know if Amie was willing to care for her half-sister.

> "I told the social worker that I was unable to care for her because of my own physical disabilities. I know that they asked me because the state tries to keep families together if they can. However, they didn't know that we did not grow up together. It was just an assumption on their part. I was notified

that my half-sister was placed in a nursing home. I felt sad about this, but there was nothing realistically I could do for her. I thought of her often and hoped that she would adjust and be OK."

Elisabeth was very girly as she began to grow. She picked out her own clothes, and loved dressing up. When Amie took her clothes shopping, she would ask: "Is this on sale?" Her closet was filled with clothes. Her favorite colors were pink and purple.

"I was so happy with caring for Elisabeth. When it was time for her to have her own room, I had Elisabeth pick out wall paper with me. Her room was wallpapered with little ballerinas and ballet slippers in a pink and purple pattern. This was such a sharp contrast to any of the rooms I lived in, but I was happy to do it."

Amie wanted Elisabeth to be a strong-minded and independent person because she did not have that kind of opportunity as a child. She hoped that Elisabeth would be able to take care of herself and not be dependent on others to the degree that she was. Playing with her brothers made her tough. "I was in awe of Elisabeth's abilities of strength and determination. In her own way, she became the boss with her brothers. They loved her, so they went along with it for the most part."

During those years, Amie continued to see Luisa to help her adjust to the changing needs of the children's development. Discipline continued to be a tough issue for Amie to accept, and she had to work hard to understand its benefits. Since she experienced harsh discipline growing up, she had trouble with going through with it. She found it hard to bear when the children gave her a hard time. When she tried to discipline them,

they would fight back. The only way she was able to stick to any discipline was when it came to their physical safety. "It was only then that I was able to put my foot down, no matter how big the tantrum."

Amie told me that she always told people that she viewed herself as the mother hen. Her little chicks were always in front of her, and she was lagging behind. "Luisa reminded me of the things I did right with the children. Sometimes I would even bring them in with me so that they could voice what was bothering them. Luisa was known as the 'worry doctor.' She was very supportive of me and my family."

> "Luisa helped fill in many of the blanks in Amie's life. She worked with me over thirteen years, to 're-grow up' properly and raise the children. I didn't always get it right, but I kept working on it. I will always be grateful to her for all the love she showed, and give her the credit for all of the hard work it took to help me. She too holds a special place in my heart for her great ability to help others."

TIME TO MOVE

The house that Amie's family was living in began to become too small for all of them. Amie and Alex began to look for another home because the boys needed a new school. They looked at various houses in different towns and finally found one about an hour away from where they were living.

> "It was a beautiful home with a bedroom for each of the children. There was plenty of back yard space for them to run around. It was also only about thirty minutes away from Alex's office. This would make his commuting time much shorter. We also had to find a new congregation to go to. As it happened, there was one recommended by a friend that was located right by the exit of the highway near the new house, only about two miles away. This new location gave the children more of an opportunity to see their cousins and grandparents on a weekly basis, something that hadn't been feasible before. It didn't take the children a long period of time to adjust. After a while we were all glad that the move had been made."

LOSING A CLOSE ALLY

When Elisabeth was three years old, Amie experienced her first significant adult loss. She learned about this through her roommate from the residence.

"Jane had called me to tell me the sad news that Mazie had died. Mazie's daughter had called Jane to let her know. Mazie told her daughter to notify her if something had happened to her because she felt that Jane was also one of her daughters. I was really shocked. I didn't believe her at first. Jane explained to me that Mazie had suffered from heart failure and didn't want me to worry about her. I just couldn't believe it. I even had a dream about Mazie dying a few years earlier, but hoped it wouldn't happen for a very long time. When I finally hung up with Jane, I cried for Mazie for a long time. My cheerleader and friend was gone! For the next several weeks, Jane and I called each other every day that to console themselves. We both felt honored and fortunate to have known such a person. Mazie was so proud of us. She made us feel strong, and unconditionally loved. She didn't always agree with our choices, but she

understood them, and helped us work through them. She knew how tough life could be and wanted us to be prepared for it."

Mazie left behind a great legacy for "her girls." Amie said that if anyone had a serious problem after she left the residence, Mazie always told them that her door was open, even though it was against the rules.

"I remember that Mazie let me sleep over in the other houseparent's room one time when I was having trouble with something. Mazie told me to exit the kitchen door and come to the front door, and ring the bell as if I was coming for a visit the following morning. Mazie came to the door and acted as if nothing ever happened. I had taken a bath in the room, and thought that my wet hair had given me away to the other girls, but who was telling who?"

Amie knows that if Mazie were here today she would be so proud of her and encourage her to keep going.

"It wasn't long after that that Jane called to tell me that Mazie's daughter Judy had been diagnosed with breast cancer. She had three children and Mazie helped her raise them, just like her mother had done for her. How sad for Mazie's daughter's children. They lost their beloved grandmother and now their mother. Mazie was seventy-two when she passed, and her daughter in her mid-forties."

Amie really felt that she had been left alone again after Mazie's passing. This made Amie think that she was now really raising her children without a mother. Mazie was not technically her mother, but she treated her as if she was her daughter. She missed her terribly. How she would have loved seeing Amie's children grow! "They would have called her Nana."

Mazie had taught her to find her own voice, and stand up for what she believed in. "The only bad thing Mazie taught me was how to curse. Mazie was really good at it. I learned it well." It took years for Amie to not curse, but it slips out when she gets really frustrated or angry. Amie told me that it helps her to "get it all out" and to express how she is really feeling. "Alex would tell you that he vehemently disagrees with me on this issue. We still debate it, especially when I use those forbidden words."

MOVING RIGHT ALONG

The boys and Elisabeth were growing up fast. They were involved in music class and after-school activities like baseball and pioneer girls. They also spent time with their classmates after school. They had many big family birthday parties themselves. They participated with their friends, who also invited them to their parties and other activities. There was also a youth group at the congregation that the children were involved in once a week. Amie felt that in order to keep her children on track, it was important to provide activities that they enjoyed. This would also help to keep them out of trouble.

Alex liked to take trips and plan vacations for the children to see things, like he did when he was growing up. Many of these trips revolved around congregational meetings held in different parts of the country, so Alex would plan excursions around them. They had the opportunity to fly places and spend lots of time in hotel pools.

Samuel was soon reaching Bar Mitzvah age. The leader of the congregation began to teach Samuel his portion almost a year before the big day. Samuel had to write his own sermon. His portion was from the book of Zechariah, chapter 12. This portion talks about how when Jerusalem is surrounded by her enemies the Messiah comes and rescues the Jewish people. He did very well. Samuel was big enough to fit into a man's suit.

He was so handsome! Amie and Alex were so proud of him. He had one special friend from school attend, along with Alex's family members. Many of their long-time friends also attended this milestone in Samuel's life. At Samuel's Bar Mitzvah party, a special cake was made to acknowledge his accomplishment.

At the same time, Amie had completed her undergraduate degree, which was a long time in coming. It took her over twenty years, on and off, to complete. She told me that she always told the children that she had to work on her "college homework," while they did theirs. She ended up receiving a Bachelor of Science in Humanities and Education degree from the state university.

A few years later, when Elisabeth was going on seven, she told Alex that she wanted another baby. He didn't want one right away, but eventually agreed to it. Alex said that he realized he was being selfish not to want another child when it was something that Amie strongly desired. Amie got pregnant soon after that discussion, and found out she was going to have another boy. Amie told me that she always wanted a "biggish" kind of family. Four children would be her limit.

LOSS OF A BABY

This pregnancy, however, turned out to be more difficult. Amie said that she really did not feel very well during this one. When Amie reached her sixth month in the pregnancy, her doctor wanted her to go for a sugar test to check for diabetes. He also wanted to do an amniocentesis, which is a test to check for birth defects. Amie told the doctors that it would not be right to terminate a pregnancy, even if something were wrong. She would leave the matter in God's hands.

Amie told me that all this discussion with the doctor caused her to worry about her pregnancy. Amie was also experiencing a constant cough that she could not take medication for because that could be harmful to the baby in her womb.

After the sugar test was completed, Amie started experiencing Braxton Hicks contractions. She really did not know what they were, so she went to the doctor. What was happening was that the baby moved all the time, and he would move to the right of her belly and it felt like a ball, then move again. The doctor suggested that Amie go for an ultrasound test, and this made her worry even more.

In the meantime, Elisabeth came down with chicken pox.

> "I was concerned that if I were to deliver the baby then, there wouldn't be anyone to look

after Elisabeth. When she was on the mend after
two weeks, something disturbing happened.
Suddenly, the baby, which had been very active,
stopped moving all together. I called the doctor
again and he told me to meet him at the hospital.
I called a friend from the congregation to tell
her what was going on, and she told me that she
would come over and watch Samuel, Benjamin
and Elisabeth while Alex and I went to the hos-
pital. She knew that it wasn't going to turn out
well, but didn't tell me."

When Amie and Alex arrived there, the doctor told them
that the baby was probably in trouble. They did a more intense
ultra sound, and found out that the baby had three knots in the
cord and had to be taken out right away to survive. The prep
for the emergency C-section went very quickly. Amie and Alex
were really scared. Alex was not even allowed in the operating
room. He went to the hospital chapel to pray. He told Amie
later that he prayed to God and asked Him that if the baby
was not healthy, to take him home to Heaven. Amie and Alex
decided that they were going to name him Aaron, which means,
"Shining light."

The baby was stillborn around 7:30 PM.

"The doctor woke me up after the surgery, and
told me that he was so sorry but the baby didn't
make it. The baby was perfectly formed, but was
totally blue because he lacked oxygen. The nurse
gave me the baby to hold, but I didn't know what
to do. The incision where the C-section took
place was really hurting. I did not know how to
touch him. He was all wrapped up in a receiving

blanket with dried amniotic fluid on him. All I could do was just look at him. He resembled Samuel and appeared like he was sleeping."

Alex took pictures of him for Amie to remember what he looked like. She has kept one of them all these years.

"I only had a few minutes, then the nurse took him away. It was too soon. The doctor also told me that he wanted to do an autopsy to check if the baby had any brain issues."

Amie said that it was all right with her because there was nothing they could do for him now. He was gone. Now he was a shining light in Heaven.

While the doctor was getting the paperwork ready, Alex's parents came into the recovery room to see the baby. "His mother held my hand and all I could say to her was, 'I'm sorry.'"

Amie told me that she had to ask a friend to stay over to take care of the children, because she wanted Alex to stay with her in the hospital so she would not be alone.

The head nurse on the ward asked Amie if she would be all right if they put her in a room by herself on the maternity floor, or if she wanted to be moved. Amie said that it was okay to put her in a room by herself. At least she did not have to share a room with a woman who had her baby with her.

It was a tough night for all of them. "I just couldn't understand why this had happened to Alex and me." She really questioned her faith, too. "I cried so hard, my heart was broken. There was no baby to hold." Amie told me that she kept questioning herself with "what if" she had done this or that, but it was to no avail.

"The next day, two nurses that had been in the operating room with her told me that I had shed some tears after the anesthesiologist put me to sleep. The nurse felt that I must have heard something that was going on. She told me she came over and talked to me quietly and told me that it was going to be all right. They also told me that there had been three knots in the chord by the baby's belly button, and that is why he had stopped moving. These knots had cut off his oxygen supply. That gave me some comfort, but I was really upset. Someone sent the social worker down to try to calm me down, and to see if I was going to be all right. As we talked, she suggested that I see a therapist to help me adjust. That made sense to me, but I wasn't convinced that the pain of it would ever go away."

A friend of Amie's named Naomi who lived an hour away from her came to visit her in the hospital.

"She brought her a few house dresses that I could wear while I was in the hospital, and stayed with me all afternoon. She was very comforting to me and reassured me that everything was going to be all right. I really didn't believe her, but was touched that she was so gentle with me. I had only brought maternity night gowns to wear in the hospital, and felt uncomfortable wearing them now that the baby was gone. Naomi let me cry with her, and that was a gift in itself that I am so grateful for."

Another married couple who were friends of Alex's also came to see Amie and tried to comfort her, but it was to no avail.

> "I was very thankful that they came to see me, but couldn't receive anything from them. It was so raw in me. I couldn't understand why this happened to me, and to be honest, no one else did either. Sure, when a relative dies, people try to say nice things about them, but what could anyone say about this? It wasn't their experience."

Most of their other close friends from the congregation came to visit and offer their condolences, as well as one of Alex's cousins who had experienced losing a baby two years before.

> "Now they really understood what I was feeling. They even brought me chocolate cookies, and told me that if I needed to talk after I left the hospital, I could call them. That was very thoughtful of them. I really didn't want them to re-live what they went through, but I was thankful that they offered such a gift. I was only allowed to stay four days after this delivery because the insurance guidelines had changed. However, this time I really didn't want to go home because I had no baby in my arms to take home with me. When I got home I cried a lot. It was a good thing that I had the boys and Elisabeth to focus on to distract me. I was on the phone a lot, talking to people who called to console me. People we knew sent me flowers. After a while the house looked like a funeral home and I got rid of them all!"

There was real emotional and spiritual work that needed to be done so that Amie would find healing to move on and come to terms with what had happened. Many of the people from their congregation who came to the hospital also cooked meals for about two weeks. "That was very thoughtful of them. After we ran out of food, it was my turn to cook. It was hard for me at first, because I really didn't want to do anything. I didn't have much of an appetite. But the children were hungry and our daily routines had to get back in order."

The children saw Amie cry and she tried to comfort them at the same time. A social worker from the hospital informed Amie that they provided a grief group for parents that had lost children in childbirth.

Amie decided that she needed someone to talk to, other than friends, to help her recover from the loss of her baby.

"I found through the grapevine a counselor near where we lived who had done this kind of work. I thought I would give her a try. She was a lovely lady and had similar religious beliefs. I ended up talking with her once a week for about nine months. One of the main issues we discussed about this loss was that I thought I was being punished. This was an automatic button that showed up for me before. The counselor explained that bad things happen to people all the time, yet in the midst of these incidents there is a God who loves us and sent his Son to die for us, and would make a way to get through these tough times. She also shared that God cries with us when He sees His children suffer. This helped me understand that God has always been there for me, even if I couldn't see it. She also said that

He will bring people to help us to keep going. The counselor gave me hope, and helped me to realize that I wasn't alone in my grief, even though I felt alone. She also shared with me that fathers grieve differently than mothers do because we are the ones who give birth to that child. She explained that this difference in grieving doesn't mean that Alex doesn't grieve, and that I should give him the same room he gives me to grieve. I thought that it was her best advice. This way we could help each other through the process, no matter how long it took."

While going to see this kind, lovely person, Amie and Alex also attended the grief group on a monthly basis at the hospital.

"It was sad to listen to other couples' stories, but we felt comforted that this occurred more commonly than anyone would suspect. After a year of going to this group, they held a special parade in town to honor those babies who didn't make it. There was also a special walkway dedicated to these babies. Each name and date of birth was engraved on a brick that was laid in this walkway at the hospital. These babies were not lost in vain. Strangely, they had a purpose. It was to go on with life in their memory."

Amie and Alex also befriended two other couples who went through this. Over the following years, they got together at Amie's family gatherings and other occasions, and have kept in touch.

"Most of the time, when something like this happens, it is normal to want another baby. People think that this done in order to replace the baby that was lost. Maybe it is on some level, but it goes deeper than that. Having a baby is a natural part of life. Babies bring hope for the future, and make life seem that everything is going to be all right. Many of these couples had more children, even though they missed the child that died. The subsequent children made their presence more precious and special for their parents."

UNLIKELY FRIENDS

Within a month or so, everyone's life went back to being as normal as possible. The children were back in school, and Amie felt that she could not stay home all day and think about what happened. She decided to look for a part-time job so that she could be home when the children came home from school. At this point, the children were 17, 13 and 8 years old. Someone suggested that she apply to work in the schools, serving lunches. Amie had done this kind of job years ago when the boys were younger, so she applied and got the job.

Amie needed to come to a meeting where all the kitchen workers would be assigned to a school for that year.

> "It turned out that I was assigned to work with a lady named Anna. She later told people that she didn't think that I would be able to do the job. In our first meeting, I brought Benjamin and Elisabeth along with me so that she could meet them. Anna told me that she had three children. I also shared with her that I had worked in the school kitchen before. As we got to know each other, I told her that I recently had a still birth, and that was one of the reasons I applied for this job. She said that she was so sorry to hear that. Anna

153

showed me around the kitchen, and informed me that there would be three lunch periods that we had to provide lunches for. It was my job to help with the preparation for the lunches, which were served on large, industrial aluminum trays. After the lunches were served, then I was to sell the snacks, which included things like chips, cookies and ice cream. In between each lunch period I was to clean the counters and stack the trays in the sink for washing. It was my job to wash all the trays and any pots that were used to cook the food.

It seemed that I would never finish, since there was always something else to wash. I always left with my belly wet, and my hands looking water-logged. Mazie would have been proud! The only task that I wasn't able to do was carry the food trays from the ovens to the counters."

Amie never took a day off. "I enjoyed being around Anna and felt like I was productive."

Anna was really impressed with Amie and later on commented that she had to "eat her words." She told Amie that she had to ask God for forgiveness because she had judged the book by its cover.

A New Blessing to the Family

B y the spring of the school year, Amie found out that she was pregnant again. The doctors had told her to wait for at least six months to give her body a chance to heal. It took nine months. Amie was so excited that she had gotten pregnant again. How appropriate that this baby was due around Thanksgiving time!

The children were happy for her and so was her friend Anna. As Amie's belly began to grow, Amie had to sit down to prepare the school lunches and sell the snacks. She was still able to wash the pots and trays, but had to be more careful so that she would not fall. Nevertheless, she was able to make it through the school year intact.

"Anna and I were able to talk about everything, including what was going on with our family members, especially the children." Anna's children were older than Amie's. "We spent Christmas together that year at Anna's house. Her children were very accepting of my children and we had a really fun time." Anna had become a fixture at Amie's house as she watched her pregnancy with this new baby.

Another close friend named Marie lived down the block from Amie. Amie had met her years back when her daughter

Elisabeth was four years old. That day Amie had to take one of the boys to the doctor, and she got home a few minutes after the bus dropped her daughter off.

> "Marie was there talking to Elisabeth as I got into the driveway. Marie and I would talk occasionally but didn't get to know each other until an acquaintance had let her know what had happened to Aaron. Marie came to the door and told me that she had found out what had happened, and wanted to be of help. From that point on, we saw each other a few times a week. Her husband was also helpful with fixing things around the house, because Alex was not handy by any means."

Marie knew that Amie was working with Anna, and they finally met each other one day after school. "I told Marie that the doctor said that I could have one more baby, and when I did get pregnant, Marie was very happy to hear the news. Marie and Anna began to become friendly and were planning what they would do to help when the baby was born. It was a team effort on both their parts."

The baby was scheduled to be born the Wednesday after Thanksgiving Weekend. Amie could not wait until she went into labor. On the following Monday morning, Amie began her labor very early around one o'clock in the morning. Amie's labor was progressing, and by six o'clock in the morning she knew that she was in real labor. "Since Anna had to go to her school early to set things up, I called her to let her know that labor had started. Anna told me that she would visit her after work."

There was an older couple who went to their congregation who were close friends to Alex and Amie. "I knew that they were early risers, and that it would be fine to call and tell them

that I was in labor. They were so excited for me and said that they would let everyone in the congregation know it, too. They asked that Alex call them know when the baby was born."

Amie knew that six o'clock was too early to wake up Marie, so she decided to get up and take a shower, get dressed and make a cup of tea before she had to wake up Samuel. He had to be at school earlier than Benjamin and Elisabeth. "I told him that I was in labor and would probably have their brother by the end of the day."

After Samuel left for school, Amie decided that eight o'clock would be a better time to inform Marie of what was going on.

"Marie had volunteered to get Benjamin and Elisabeth on the school bus and would be at my house if I needed her to get them off the bus later that afternoon. If everything worked out all right, Alex would be home when Benjamin and Elisabeth got home from school. This was such a thoughtful thing for her to do. She was excited for me and told me that she would pray, and that the baby would be fine. By seven thirty in the morning, I called the doctor to let him know that I was in labor. He told me to get to the hospital as soon as I was able."

Amie got Benjamin and Elisabeth up and dressed. They ate breakfast and got their book bags ready. "I told them that by the end of the school day, their brother would be born. Alex also was getting ready to go to the hospital. By eight thirty, Marie arrived, gave me a big hug, and asked Alex to call her when the baby was born. Then we left for the hospital. When I arrived at the hospital, the doctor examined me and told his staff to

begin the prep needed to get this baby born as soon as possible. I was going to have an epidural. The funny thing was that I could hear all of the chatter going on as to how to start the C-Section. The doctors were discussing the initial incision. They wanted to do an up and down incision."

In all of her past deliveries, Amie had gotten what was called a bikini cut.

"I interrupted them and suggested that one scare was enough for me to deal with and convinced them to use the same one for the incision. They agreed, and the surgery went on without a hitch."

When the baby was delivered, around ten fifty in the morning, "I heard his cry and it made me cry, too. Alex asked them who was going to do the *bris*. They all said in unison that we should get a *moil*." *Bris* is a Hebrew word for circumcision. A *moil* is a religious Jewish man who is trained in doing circumcisions and has to be certified by the state. Circumcision is traditionally done on the eighth day after a baby boy is born. It turns out that a baby's blood clots best on that day, which means that that there is less bleeding when the procedure is done then. The *moil* is mostly used by orthodox Jewish families. It is a quicker procedure than what is done in the hospital, and it is less painful.

"After the doctors checked the baby's vitals, and said that everything was fine, Alex and I breathed a sigh of relief. The baby weighed eight pounds and eight ounces, and was nineteen inches long. We decided to name him Seth. It means, 'Appointed substitute.' The nurse went over to me to show me the baby. He looked different from the other

children. I gave him a kiss. Then she took him to the nursery to clean him up, and I was wheeled into the recovery room. Alex followed me, but in a few minutes he left to call everyone in the family and let them know that Seth was finally here."

After about an hour, Amie was bought up to her room, and Seth was brought up to see her. "I was so excited that all I could do was look at him and cry tears of relief." Amie told me that she had prayed to God to give her one more chance to have a child to raise, and he granted her request. Amie exclaimed: "I was so thankful!"

This final time around, Amie was more comfortable about what she was able to do for Seth. "The nursing staff at the hospital helped me when I needed it. They allowed me to keep Seth in the bed with me with the side rails up so that I could nurse him on demand and change his diapers."

When Alex and the children came to visit, "I instructed them to wash their hands, and then they could hold Seth." Samuel was old enough to bring his brother and sister to see the baby because he was driving now. The Wednesday that he was supposed to be born, there was a snowstorm. Amie was glad that he was born when he was, so that now he was safe with her.

Unlike the other times she had given birth, Amie could only stay in the hospital for four days, so going home was a little rough. She had not gotten her "sea legs" yet, so the walker really came in handy. "Everyone pitched in to help care for Seth. Samuel liked to hold and carry him. However, he didn't like changing diapers that much because Seth peed on him!" Benjamin and Elisabeth took charge. They carried him, help bath him, dressed him and held him. They only gave him over to Amie to nurse him. He was a good nurser, like his siblings.

Alex and Amie decided that they would wait eight days to have Seth circumcised. They found a *moil* who agreed to do it for them. During this time, Amie met another young woman and her family who would later become close friends. Her name was Lorraine. She had a baby five months older than Seth. His name was Jesse. She was married and had a daughter Benjamin's age.

Lorraine came over to help Amie get showered and dressed for the *bris*. Amie was still having difficulty getting around due to the C-section. Marie and her husband came over to help, as well. Alex's family was there and his father was selected to hold Seth in honor of who he was as the elder statesman of the family. "I was a bit nervous, and when it was done, Seth cried, and so did I." Anna, her husband, and close friends, were invited to this joyous family occasion. All went well.

Seth became the center of attention for the family. Everyone rallied around Amie to care for him. Anytime he cried, there was always someone there to pick him up. "I didn't like to see him cry. Within a few months I figured out that Seth really yelled more than he cried. There weren't any tears yet. Even so, we all took very good care of him. Seth was a good baby. As he grew in personality he smiled a lot."

Amie told me that Marie would come over in the late morning to help bathe him in the kitchen sink. After work, Anna would come and see what he was up to. She thought he was adorable. Amie was very willing to share Seth with any of their friends, because she was so glad that he was there.

When Seth was about three months old, Amie and Alex wanted to have a dedication service for him. Alex's family attended this service. Afterwards, the congregation had a special cake that had been made for this occasion.

There was also another local congregation which Amie and Alex occasionally attended who wanted to do the same for Seth. They had a special service for baby dedications. Many of Amie

and Alex's friends that attended there knew what happened when they lost Aaron, and they wanted to see Seth. It was such a lovely moment. "Now Seth was doubly blessed," Amie said.

Amie and Alex both felt that having Seth restored their family. His birth brought forth healing for all. No one expected to lose a baby. Having this experience had taught Amie's family that one does not always get what one wants in life. Bad things do not happen just because someone is bad, necessarily, but because it is part of life. No one gets everything right, or bypasses pain or heartache. Hopefully joy, peace and happy times outweigh the bad times.

Like his siblings, Seth walked and started saying words after his first birthday. By the time he was two and a half, Anna suggested putting training pants on him to see if he was interested in getting potty trained.

> "He didn't take to it right away, but by the summer he trained himself. He liked to run around in his birthday suit! He didn't like wearing a diaper anymore, and we all called him a 'big boy.' Benjamin and Elisabeth enjoyed taking care of Seth when they were home from school. Benjamin showed Seth how to play video games, and Elisabeth taught him to roller skate toddler style."

By the time Seth was two years and nine months old, Amie put him in pre-school for a full day, so that he would not be bored. He really enjoyed it, and came home with such enthusiasm. Lorraine's son also attended there, and they became friends. Life was busy and everyone had their own schedule.

The boys were finishing up junior and senior high school. Elisabeth was about to go to junior high school. Elisabeth, like her brothers, began to prepare for her Bat Mitzvah when she

was eleven years old. It was traditional for girls to have their Bat Mitzvah at twelve years old.

> "I took Elisabeth shopping for a pretty dress, with shoes to match. We found a dress that had a flowered lace design. I found a pants outfit for me to match the color of Elisabeth's dress. We both were dressed in ivory. Elisabeth had beautiful long hair and wore a flowered headband to show it off. She learned her Scripture portion, and invited her close friends to the service and the party."

She looked so beautiful, and Amie and Alex were so proud of her!

As Samuel was about to finish high school, he really didn't know what he wanted to do, Amie shared.

> "I suggested that he go to the local community college and take classes so that he could look and see if anything sparked an interest. He found that he liked the math classes. I didn't want him to just stay at home, or just work at a job. The most important thing for Samuel was to have some kind of structure, keep busy and see what he would like to be. He also had a small group of friends that came over to the house frequently to hang out together. They kept in touch with each other through their milestones of growing up. Samuel was a loyal friend to his real friends — and still is to this very day."

A short time later, Samuel met someone who taught him some skills in the financial realm. He really enjoyed it, and decided to pursue it. He became his own boss and went full steam ahead and was very successful. Amie has always been proud of Samuel's determination to complete something when he puts his mind to do it. He was setting a course for himself and his future. He moved out of the house and went to live on his own with a couple of buddies of his. He worked hard and stuck with it.

Benjamin was a good student, and was also a social butterfly. Most of his friends were girls. He had some guy friends, but a few of them got in trouble for minor things. He participated in a special program in high school to see how interested he was in some aspect of medicine as a possible career. However, once he saw blood that was it! He decided that the field of medicine was not for him. He would have to look elsewhere. He always liked art and video games. He decided that when it was his turn to go to college, he would pursue something with art.

THE TWENTY-FIFTH YEAR

Alex and Amie reached a very significant milestone in their lives — they were married for twenty-five years. "I always wanted a real wedding, since we got married by the justice of the peace." Faye and Nate, an older couple in their congregation, offered Amie and Alex the use of the community room at their complex for the renewal of vows and reception. Amie was so excited! She and Alex started making plans. They decided that their oldest son Samuel would be their best man, Benjamin would be a groomsman, Elisabeth would be the maid of honor, and little Seth would be the ring bearer.

"Elisabeth and I went looking for a real wedding dress at a local bridal shop. It just so happened that she was having a sidewalk sale on the very same weekend that we went to look." Elisabeth wanted to help Amie find the perfect dress.

"As I was trying on various ones, Elisabeth found a real feminine-looking one with a scoop neck. It had previously been owned by someone else, but I didn't care. I was so excited that Elisabeth found this dress for me since she was twelve at the time. It needed some alterations, and the front needed to be a bit shorter so that I wouldn't trip over it. The owner of the store said that the dress would be

cleaned, and it would look like new. It was a beautiful dress, for sure."

Amie decided that because Alex's favorite color was blue, she wanted Elisabeth and the boys to be dressed in blue. The lady at the bridal shop found a royal blue dress for Elisabeth. When she tried it on, she looked beautiful. For the boys, Amie went to a local wedding rental place to look for them to get black suits with royal blue vests and ties. Amie wanted everything to match. The boys looked great when they tried on their suits, especially little Seth.

The hardest part of making this wedding reception was where to place everyone at the tables. Amie wanted to make sure that everyone was comfortable with whom they were placed at their table. It took a lot of thought and going over many times. The community room could hold up to 150 people. The food had to be ordered, as well as the table linens and dishes. Amie used one particular company for her family's parties at the house, and decided to use them for this big event. One of the most important things she wanted for this reception was a *chuppah* (a Jewish wedding canopy) to renew their vows under. This company had one. It had a red velvet covering with tassels held together with four wooden poles.

Amie also needed people to serve the food and take pictures. Her friend Anna suggested that her girls would be willing to do the job if Amie was willing to hire them. Of course, Amie said that she would hire them.

Everything went off without a hitch. Amie, Elisabeth and the boys looked great. A few days before the big day, all the boys got their hair cut. On the day of the ceremony, early in the morning, Amie and Elisabeth got their hair and nails done.

Two hours before the wedding Amie and the children, along with Anna, came to the community room to set everything up. The room looked elegant. Lorraine made candle center pieces

in navy blue, and she made all the flowers for the family members. They were so pretty and delicate. The boys and Alex had flowers on the lapels of their suits. Amie, Elisabeth and the flower girl each had a bouquet of flowers. Lorraine also made them for Alex's parents.

Nate and Faye stood in and gave Amie away to Alex. They loved Amie's family. Every time they would see Amie or her family members, they would say things like, "You are so blessed to have wonderful children." They both recently passed away within a couple years of each other. This couple was considered the grandparents of the children that went to the congregation — kind of like an extended family.

Alex made sure that Amie invited people they knew from earlier years, including the person who married them. Everyone that was invited came to this reception. Amie's children were very involved with the ceremony. The flower girl, Lynn, and little Seth walked down to the *chuppah* first. They looked so cute! Lynn's mom had found a dress that had a royal blue top, attached to an off-white skirt. It was so feminine and girly. After the vows were spoken, little Seth asked to give Mommy the ring. The boys began the blessings for Amie and Alex, and helped their father do the traditional breaking of the glass with his foot.

Amie and Alex were so happy! It was a wonderful event. She told me that she did not remember eating very much because she was so happy that everyone was having such a good time, including her. This was a dream come true. For the first time, she finally felt like a bride.

This was an event that was truly memorable. It was a real milestone for Amie and her family. A foundation had been laid that could not be broken. Amie could now say that she had a family of her own. She wasn't missing out on anything anymore. Life could only get better from this point on.

Obtaining a Master's Degree

Amie went back to college on a part-time basis, taking night classes so she could obtain a Master's degree in Social Work. Amie felt that due to all of her experiences in foster care, she might be able to help someone else on a professional level. She had gotten a recommendation for a social work school from Luisa, but after the first semester she was forced to leave. She was not able to keep a B average. She was two points shy of it. "One of the professors suggested that I go back to school and get a Bachelor's degree. How stupid was that? I already had one!" The strange thing was that this school was not very supportive of Amie's learning disabilities. "Wasn't that part of being a social worker? All they had to do was make a few accommodations for me and I would have succeeded there."

Amie found out that there was another school in her area that had a similar degree program that took three years to complete. As a matter of fact, this was the school where she had started her college career over twenty years previously. Amie went for an interview and asked if they would admit her as a student who, due to her learning disability, would only take one class at a time. They agreed, and in the fall of that year she resumed her pursuit of a Master's degree.

Amie experienced some of the same frustrations with retaining the information that she had before, but this time around there was a computer to help her.

> "I would read the textbooks, then type what I understood them to say. It took hours of work, but I felt that I was able to participate more in class because I understood the work better. Many times the children would come home from school and wonder what I was doing. It seemed to them that I was always at the computer and other things, like making dinner, would have to wait."

Amie also met two wonderful people in her Master's classes. One was named Jenny, and another named Karen. "Karen became my study partner. We worked on class projects, term papers and studied for exams together. She also had two children. One was Elisabeth's age, and the other Seth's age."

This time around, her grades were much higher. She was able to keep more than a B average. There was a requirement that she do internships so as to gain experience in various fields. One of them was working with pre-school children, and the other was with children who needed outside support for the family, such as the Big Brothers and Big Sisters program.

After she completed these internships, Amie had made some changes to the classes she needed to graduate with because the school was changing the program. The course work was going to be done with shorter semesters, which required less time for the required reading. "I only had a few more classes to take in order to finish the program. I spoke with my advisor and we arranged these classes so that I would finish on time."

Before graduation, Amie was required to take a comprehensive exam. This exam could be thought of like a bar exam

after law school. If you passed, then you could graduate and receive the Master's degree credit. Amie asked if she would be allowed to take this exam with a proctor using the computer because of her visual disability. The chairman of the department agreed and she was given extra time to complete this exam. She passed! Amie was able to graduate with a thirty-six credit Master's degree in Guidance and Counseling. "Now I had the paper to back me up with a job in a profession that I was suited for." Alex and the children were so proud of her. "They cheered at my graduation ceremony when my name was called."

WORK YEARS

Over the years, Amie worked odd jobs to help bring money into her household. Before she finished graduate school, Amie worked in a local nursing home in the evenings till one in the morning on a part-time basis. Seth was about three years old at the time. Benjamin and Elisabeth helped Alex take care of him and put him to bed. He liked their company, and did not mind Amie being out of the house.

After graduation and finishing her last internship, the director from one of the internships asked Amie if she would be willing to work for her agency, which helped at-risk children. "This would be my first professional job. The person I was working under had left, and I was to take up where he had left off."

In the beginning, things were going along fine. Yet after a while, Amie became a bit overwhelmed with certain demands of the job. One of these demands was driving to clients' homes. Amie had difficulty driving to places that she was unfamiliar with because of her visual learning disabilities. Amie decided to leave because she didn't want to make waves with the director. She was not very confident of her position, and there were things that went on in the office she was not comfortable with. She was really green to office politics.

In the late spring of that year, a friend from graduate school called her with a possible job offer for someone she worked with at another facility. This position would be working with low income senior citizens. It was a part-time position, and the work schedule would be flexible. Amie interviewed for the job, and two months later she was hired. This was a better fit for her. She was by herself in an office, and the clients came to her for assistance. She did not have to drive from place to place. It was stationary. There were occasional meetings with the director of the program, but Amie was on her own and could work at her own pace.

> "My friend Jan came over to the job site to help me with the documentation that was required for the main office once a month. The best way I was able to organize the information was to create a chart. This way I would remember what happened with the clients, and translate the chart information into a monthly report. I really learned a lot about what it meant to be a senior citizen and many of the clients and I got along really well. It was my job to help the clients with anything that related to their living or personal issues."

After five years on the job, things began to change. The director of the program was retiring and a new director had been found. He brought his own changes, and things were not as comfortable as they were before.

> "I made a great effort to stick it out until Elisabeth and Seth were out of school. Up to that point I had held down this job for almost eight years. However, there were a few major issues that

arose that I was not willing to deal with. Also, at times the learning disability got in the way and the director really didn't understand what I was faced with. He wanted changes that I was not able to produce."

It was a difficult decision to make. She did not want to leave the clients, especially those with whom she had developed a close relationship with.

"The director offered me the opportunity to take a leave of absence to see if I would be willing to come back to work. After the time was up, the reasons I left in the first place were still there. Nothing had changed. There were other issues going on in my personal life which made it inconvenient to do so. I missed working with the clients for a long time after I left, but I still felt that on the whole I did help people and learned a lot from them."

This work experience taught Amie a lot. Through it all, she learned that she was as smart as the next person. Amie was good at helping people, and that made her feel good about herself. She had touched their lives, and they had touched hers. Amie learned that the work world was tough, and many times you cannot make your colleagues your friends.

"You need to remind yourself that what the job is does not matter so much as who you are as a person. Everyone needs to work to the best of their ability. Mistakes are inevitable, but the motive is what really counts. Sometimes it can't

be helped. Not everyone will agree with your approach. The most important thing is that you be honest, and have a positive attitude as much as possible. The ability to work is a very important aspect of success in life. Everyone has a place and a calling. It is up to us to find out what that is. So in the meantime, you may have to take a job that you may not like, but it should only be looked at as a temporary move. Keep your eyes and ears open for better opportunities, as well as study to make improvements. Most importantly, keep checking how much your heart is in it. The more the heart is in it, the more enjoyable working will be. The ability to work and hold down a job is only part of what makes a life worth living."

A New Life Stage

While Amie was still working, she was focused on fitting things in around the children's school schedule, as well as her physical therapy sessions and piano lessons. Meanwhile, life in the home began to change. Her children were growing into young adults. She knew that one day they would all be out of the house and on their own.

Samuel was getting ready to live on his own. He had a job that could afford him that possibility. Benjamin was in college, and Seth was this little boy who was growing up and running around to get everyone's attention. Elisabeth was still in high school, soon to turn sweet sixteen. She wanted to have a party.

"Elisabeth had a few close girlfriends from school and the congregation. Alex and Amie picked out a place to have the party and the plans were underway. Elisabeth picked out a new dress, of course, with matching shoes to add to her collection. All of the girls she invited got dressed up, too, but Elisabeth was the prettiest of them all! Some of Samuel's friends came to the party and met their future spouses there. Benjamin enjoyed parties, and danced with all the girls. Seth just

ran around with Jesse and did not pay attention to anyone."

It was a very special milestone for Amie, as well as Elisabeth. Her "daughter girl" was growing up into a very lovely young lady. Amie's children were becoming young adults, and Alex's and her influence was about to change.

All Grown up and Going to the Castle

Samuel was on his own supporting himself, and even had been so successful that he was able to buy his own home at age 22. A little while later, he met a very pretty young lady through his cousin. His cousin and this young lady had become friends in high school, and she introduced her friend to Samuel. Her name was Ann. When they met, Ann was in college. They soon became smitten with each other. After Ann graduated from college, their relationship began to become serious. Amie remembers talking with Samuel about his future plans. He came over to the house to talk to his dad, informing him that he wanted to marry Ann.

Samuel asked Amie if she would go with him to pick out the ring. Amie always told her boys that they should buy a good "rock," at least a carat in size. Samuel followed her instructions, and picked out a stunning ring. "Ann liked this particular cut of diamond and Samuel wanted her to have it. It was beautiful!"

After the ring was purchased, the plan was to show Ann's parents, and ask them for her hand in marriage.

> "When we arrived at their home, they were ecstatic. Her mother asked me, 'You love my girl?'

I responded, "Of course." Ann's father had a big smile and kind of giggled. He said he knew what Samuel was up to, and with a handshake and a hug, gladly gave his permission."

Now it was time to make wedding plans. The first big event would be an engagement party. They decided to host it at Amie and Alex's home in their backyard. It was a very special party.

"The weather was tenuous, and during the party it rained all day about as hard as I'd ever seen. It literally came down in torrents all day long and into the night when we had the party. Thank goodness there was a party tent in our backyard to cover everyone, but the rain was so heavy that water began to come in under the tent. Benjamin was very helpful in getting bales of hay to keep the water out. In spite of the rain, Samuel and Ann wanted to have sparklers. When they went off, part of the tent's roof had to be moved so the smoke could go up to the sky. It could have caused a fire, but everything was fine. The food was great, and all the invited guests remarked that it was the best engagement party ever. I guess you could say that the heavy rain was like showers of blessings."

Samuel and Ann went to look at a lot of places for the wedding ceremony and reception, Amie told me. "They finally picked their 'castle' to get married in." The wedding ceremony and reception would take place there. The leader from Samuel's youth group would officiate the ceremony. It was a small place, and the ceremony was held in one room, followed by the reception in another room. Everyone who was invited came to the

wedding. Amie told me that she never thought that she would be dancing with a tall, dark and handsome man in the middle of a castle. This was her first time to show off to Samuel during the mother-son dance. After the dance, she had the best seat in the house by the front tables. She could see all the action.

All of the girls in the bridal party, including Elisabeth and Samuel's cousin, looked beautiful. The guys in the bridal party were so very handsome. Most of them were Samuel's friends from high school. They, along with their wives, still keep in touch with each other. Benjamin was his best man and gave the seven Jewish blessings. Everyone was so supportive of them and wished them well. Samuel found a good wife and obtained "favor from the Lord." It was a beautiful wedding and Samuel and Ann outdid themselves. Amie and Alex were so proud of them.

THE SPANISH VILLA

Amie and Alex's second child Benjamin found his mate and got married three years after Samuel and Ann got married. What a romantic story! It all began in the fall, four years earlier, when he had gone down to Florida for a youth rally called Grass Roots. He called Amie during this conference and said that he noticed this lovely young woman and said that she could be a "possibility." Her name was Ileana.

> "I asked him why he thought such a thing. He said that she was interested in just talking to him, and vice a versa. '*Hmm*, I thought. *Maybe she is the one for him.*' In the meantime, when Benjamin came home, his friend encouraged him to just call her and see what would happen. That was the beginning. He told me that the phone calls were sweet, and I saw a smile on his face. They eventually became longer conversations that went into the night. Soon, Benjamin booked a flight to Florida to go and visit Ileana to see if the chemistry was there and if their values were similar and to see if they could go further with their relationship."

Amie told me that she and Alex were rooting for him and this sweet girl. As this relationship progressed, Amie and Alex got acquainted with Ileana's parents over the phone.

> "They were such an honest and funny couple. They really loved their daughter very much. Benjamin said that her parents were mirror images of his parents. Alex and I, along with Ileana's parents, made arrangements to meet each other. It went very well. It seemed that Benjamin's assessment was correct."

Benjamin's relationship got to the point that he wanted to get engaged.

> "I went with Benjamin to look for rings. One of our friends was a jeweler, and was very fond of Benjamin. Benjamin picked out a beautiful mount for the almost perfect stone. The jeweler said that he would put it together for Benjamin as soon as possible so that he could give it to Ileana. He was so excited! It was fun watching Benjamin make this choice in a ring. He asked me what I thought of it, and I told him it was perfect. It took two tries for Benjamin to propose to Ileana. When he did it the first time, Ileana said that she wasn't ready. Within a couple of months of talking back and forth, Benjamin felt that Ileana was ready to say yes. This time I wanted to be there when he proposed to her to make sure it stuck. Benjamin talked to her parents and decided to make a surprise visit and propose to

her. They were all excited with this idea and were fully behind it."

Amie went down to Florida with Benjamin. Ileana said yes! This was in May. Now they needed to plan for a wedding day. They wanted to get married right away and thought that Columbus Day weekend would be good time, but they later moved up the date to Labor Day weekend because everything worked out better for that weekend.

It was stressful finding the wedding place, caterer, and all the things that go with planning a wedding, Amie told me. She wanted to make both families happy. "It took a lot of work and patience to make their day happen. There were times that each of us as parents said to Benjamin and Ileana that maybe they should elope! But it was too late... they wanted a wedding." So Amie and Ileana's mother went hunting for a place. They found it — a Spanish villa. It had two big rooms, one for the ceremony and one for the reception.

Amie and Benjamin went down to Florida a few times before the wedding to get things in order. Finally, the weekend came for the wedding. It turned out that they had close to 150 people come to this joyous occasion.

"Benjamin and Ileana wanted everyone there who was important to their lives so that they could share what the Lord had done in bringing them together. The best way to describe the wedding was to say that it was truly lovely. Benjamin's older brother and younger brother were his best men, while his sister was a bridesmaid. Ileana's only sister was her maid of honor. Her brother was one of the groomsmen. There were two other friends as groomsmen, as well as, bridesmaids. Of

course, they had their proud parents to give them away in the Jewish tradition of both of them walking their daughter down to the altar which was under the *chuppah* (wedding canopy)."

The reception was really fun. Amie told me that everyone danced, told jokes, met new people and enjoyed the food. It was a wonderful wedding.

Now Amie and Alex's second oldest son and his new bride were on their way to a new life, filled with love, devotion, fun and mutual understanding that they could make a good future for each other together. Like his brother Samuel, Benjamin had found a good wife and obtained favor from the Lord. (see Proverbs 18: 22).

A Minor Interruption

After this wonderful wedding, something was going to happen that would affect all of Amie's immediate family members and take everyone off life's track. No one really saw this coming. It did not manifest itself until the late fall, and lasted for a good four months before life was able to move forward again. Alex got very sick and everything, practically speaking, came to a screeching halt.

Alex was showing signs of having a nervous breakdown. Up to this point, Alex seemed invincible. He was always busy doing his work for his clients, as well as helping others. He did *pro bono* work with prisoners for over thirty years. He would write letters of encouragement to help them stay on the right path and in faith. He also made many trips to various states to visit them. Over the years some of them would be released, and he would help them out financially as well. There was one particular person that he got involved with way too much. Alex always had issues with going a bit overboard. He was such a generous person. In this particular instance, the mother of the prisoner put a real scare in him. This started the ball rolling toward Alex having the breakdown. As it turned out nothing came of it, but Alex couldn't stop himself, nor was he able to put the brakes on it.

Along with that, his work and livelihood began to falter. He wasn't able to pay attention to what he needed to do, and financially things were out of control. He began to behave in ways that were not like him. This was compounded by lack of sleep, and he dove into an unrealistic world filled with unrealistic fears. He was only able to sleep an hour at a time, two tops. He needed medical and psychological help. Amie was afraid that she was going to lose him. "I tried to keep things under control at home, but it wasn't working. Alex was acting weird."

Amie took Alex to four doctors, all of whom prescribed medication that did not work. Some professional people in her congregation came alongside her and tried to persuade her that he needed to be hospitalized, especially because he was so sleep deprived. "He would wake up in a panic because he was having nightmares. I would try to get him to go back to sleep, but he wouldn't because of the nightmares. So during the day he would sleep because he was so exhausted. I couldn't leave him alone, or let him go anywhere by himself." It was becoming too much for Amie to handle alone.

Amie really did not want to put him in a hospital, she told me, because "I was concerned how Alex would react because he never had had that kind of experience before." However, it became more difficult to control Alex's behavior. Alex had always been such an optimistic person, and was strong in faith. He wasn't anymore, and was not making sense. It started to affect Seth. He was still in high school and it was not a good thing for him. "I notified his school and told the guidance counselor what was going on, and asked for her support for Seth. She said that she would talk with him if he wanted."

Amie finally found some help for Alex after a lot of phone calls and researching in the phone book. The hardest part for Amie was letting go. The older children were there to help, even though they too wondered if their father was going to

come back to them. "Samuel, his wife, Elisabeth, Benjamin and his wife tried to organize Alex's office before he left, but Alex messed it up after I went to sleep. It was awful."

Benjamin helped Amie get Alex to the hospital, but it turned out to be the wrong one than was originally decided upon. Amie broke down herself and cried. "I wanted to move him, but was advised not to because it would be too disruptive to him, and for what he was suffering from he would get the same treatment. I felt like I had failed, but maybe now he would at least get some sleep."

Amie shared with me that placing Alex in the hospital took place just a few days before Thanksgiving.

> "The doctor on call reassured me that Alex would be examined and receive the proper medications to help him feel better. It didn't happen right away because they were short-staffed due to the holiday. I asked the admitting doctor if they could help him with his ADHD, but she said that the hospital didn't treat that. He was going to be treated for anxiety, depression and a thought disorder which could cause him to think of committing suicide. How scary! Here this bright man was reduced to such a low point. Everyone who knew him was frightened."

"Thanksgiving was so strange. Alex wasn't there." Amie thought of Alex's mom, who was a widow and ninety-two at that time. She kind of understood what it was like for her without her husband. Samuel's wife made it a wonderful day. She cooked everything beautifully. Amie joked with her that after this ordeal was finally over, everyone would take turns

doing Thanksgiving. They all laughed. Towards the evening the older children took a plate of food with them to see their father.

> "Alex really appreciated that. He didn't like being there, and said that he didn't get to see a doctor yet. I was so upset. I didn't realize that he wouldn't be seen until the following Monday. All the staff could do was keep him comfortable. We really didn't understand that this was how things were done. Most of the time Alex complained that he slept too much. He was worried about his cases and wanted to go home. He thought that he was never going to get out of there. I tried to reassure him that the insurance would only let him stay for two weeks, tops. He didn't believe me. Alex was so angry at me. I felt so bad."

By this point, Alex's sister and her family knew what was going on. Amie tried to keep it from them, but felt that maybe they could help. Her sister-in-law was very supportive. No one wanted to tell Alex's mother. It would have been too upsetting for her.

Amie told me that Alex ended up staying there for nine days.

> "Just like I told Alex. I was given instructions to find a local clinic for follow up care. I was so glad that Alex was out of the hospital, but my work was not done. I still had to keep an eye on him, and I wasn't feeling safe enough to leave him alone. He still had a lot of anxiety about his cases, but he didn't feel strong enough to start back to work. That worried me, but I wanted to see him get better. He still was not on the right

medications, but he was able to sleep some, more than before."

I asked Amie what happened next. She told me that:

"Samuel and Elisabeth took over the logistics of his business and re-scheduled appointments for him. I had had trouble taking calls for him because I didn't have the right answers to the questions, and I didn't want anyone to know about what happened to Alex. It was overwhelming. So Samuel's wife took that task over. It must have been so hard on them. Added to that, I was not able to visit Alex unless I got a ride because I was not able to drive on the highway."

Amie wondered how Alex would come back to himself. His business was in disarray. Would Alex be able to resume things as they were before or would her life change and continue to go in the opposite direction? Alex had been such a hard worker. Amie did not quite know what to expect and was becoming too absorbed in Alex's thinking.

"I did make an appointment with an outpatient clinic, but was uncomfortable working with the staff there. I finally was able to reach one of the doctors I had contacted before Alex went to the hospital and made an appointment to see him. He said that he could help Alex and agreed to see him. After our initial visit, the doctor scheduled weekly meetings with him to work on helping Alex feel better about himself and move forward. I went with Alex to these weekly appointments,

and the doctor was able to wean Alex off the anxiety and depression medications. Alex finally got tested for ADHD and passed with flying colors! That meant that Alex exhibited Attention Deficit Hyperactivity Disorder. I was a bit more relieved that Alex could finally get help with this."

A friend told Amie that for most people with ADHD, psychological medications do not work. Only medication prescribed for ADHD works in the long run. With that kind of information under her belt, she felt that Alex must get that kind of medication.

The doctor informed Amie and Alex that there were new kinds of medications for this and that it would be beneficial for Alex to try it. This particular one worked well with the hyperactivity part. "Alex was very reluctant, and the doctor left that decision up to him. I insisted that he try it to see if it really could help him. My focus was helping Alex get on track to the road of recovery."

Amie told me that once he took the first pill, Alex was a different person. Amie doesn't think that Alex realized that the medication was also used to treat anxiety and depression.

"Alex became calmer, and easier to talk to. He even told me that his mind wasn't in racing mode anymore, and he felt at peace. He finally was coming back to the old Alex. I was so relieved. I could breathe again. The doctor suggested that Alex continue taking the medication and find a counselor to talk to in order to get readjusted to the demands of his work and everyday life. We found someone we had known from a local congregation and she was wonderful. She helped

both Alex and I work on issues together. It took about five months for Alex to get back to his old self, even though he still didn't like the fact that he was on medication. I tried to convince him that it wasn't a bad thing. It just so happened that around that time a married couple, who were friends of ours, and the husband was a psychologist, came to see us just to have time with Alex. He explained to him that it he would be all right, and that it didn't mean he lacked faith because of it. He also informed Alex that the thought disorder was really the ADHD. With that said, I felt better, and at least Alex heard it from someone he respected. Alex then was willing to continue to take [the pills] until he felt he could better handle things. He took them for a period of six months, slowly being weaned to a lower dose. He wanted to be off the medication as soon as possible. He came home from a meeting with the doctor and told me that he was finally off, but I felt he should still be on it. The doctor gave us another bottle of his medication, just in case he needed it again. He told Alex to call him if or when that happened. I kept the bottle for over a year. When the expiration date was over, I threw it out. Alex felt that he didn't need it because he had more control over the kinds of situations that got him ill in the first place."

In the midst of this whole ordeal, Amie told me a story. As she monitored Alex before he was hospitalized and after, Alex was experiencing anxiety attacks where his body would shake, especially his legs.

"I was so surprised that he was still able to drive and do errands, including picking up Seth from school that was more than thirty minutes away. Alex told me that the physical part of it didn't really bother him as much as the mental part. Underneath it all, Alex was strong as an ox. He could have come down with any other kind of illness due to the stress or even had a heart attack."

Amie told me that Alex believes that God made a way for him and his family from the Scripture verse which states: "No temptation has overtaken you except such as is common to man; but God is faithful, who will not allow you to be tempted beyond what you are able, but with temptation will also provide a way of escape, that you may be able to bear it," (see 1 Corinthians 10:13).

"Alex tells people now that he is a new man. He has made a promise to himself that nothing is so dire that it deserves that kind of negative attention. He never wants to go back there ever again, and with God's help he won't have to."

LOSING ANNA

Sadly, after a strong battle with cancer, Amie's dear Anna was gone. Little did they know how much their lives would be affected by one another from their first meeting over eighteen years before.

Anna was a strong, opinionated and very knowledgeable person. She was very matter of fact, yet very loving to those who were close to her. She talked loud, and liked to laugh. Whenever she would visit Amie at the house, there was always something going on, and she would say that it was funny, or that it gave her a headache. She enjoyed watching all the business of Amie's children, and especially Alex. "When we originally met, Anna's three children were almost grown and out of the house. Mine were not quite there yet."

"I liked talking to Anna. She was truthful, as well as encouraging." Anna admired Amie for all of her hard work, and found her story very interesting. Amie respected Anna for her direct ways, and wished that she was more like her.

Anna's husband also liked Amie and Alex. Once in a while they would go out to eat together. Most of their time was spent at each other's homes. "Anna didn't spend too much time cooking. Her husband would say that Anna fed him with the left over school food, and laughed. He didn't care, as long as she was there."

When Amie found out about the cancer, she and Alex were away at a congregational conference.

"Anna called me very early in the morning and told me that the doctor had found cancer in her pancreas. She had been scheduled for an operation to repair something, which they did, but to their surprise they found cancer, too. All I could do was tell Anna that I loved her and would be praying for her."

This was such a shock. Amie did not want to lose another special friend. She wanted to grow old with her and talk about their grandchildren.

> "Anna was a trooper. She found the course of treatment she wanted to take and went for it. Anna told me that most of us will experience cancer in our lifetime. I didn't want to believe that. I think it was her way of coming to terms with it so that she could deal with it. Anna told me, 'I'm going to fight this with all I have for as long as I have.' Those of us who knew her from working and being her friend really had hope for her that she would be one of the ones who could beat it and win. Anna had the guts to fight and not give in."

It was a battle that would last a little over two years. Towards the end, Amie suspected that things were getting worse because Anna stopped keeping in touch through emails.

> "Some of the time she would ask for her friends to pray for her if she was having a down day. Most of the time she was the encourager. I hadn't heard from her for over a few weeks, so I decided to call her husband and check in with him and see

what was going on. I really didn't expect bad news, but I thought it would be. He told me that she wasn't doing very well, and the tumors were growing and the medication to shrink them was not working anymore. It was just a matter of time. He said that Anna didn't want anyone to see how she was doing and if she had some strength she would email us, but I only received one e-mail that didn't make sense. I knew she was coming to the end. I felt so sad that my friend wouldn't finish the fight with success. Anna's husband was accepting the end as God's will because Anna was in so much pain. I didn't know this, but Anna was transferred by ambulance to the local hospice center because she didn't have much time left. As a matter of fact, I had a feeling that I should call [her husband] to see if anything had changed. He didn't pick up the phone and I knew that something was wrong. He did eventually call me back and tell me to meet him at the hospice center. Anna was there and so were all her children. They were in waiting mode for her to go."

This was very difficult for Amie.

"I didn't want to have to say goodbye to my friend. Anna's husband took my hand and walked me down to her room for me to see her one last time. I spoke softly to her and told her it was me. She didn't recognize me and only called for her husband. Her children were in and out of her room, trying to console each other. I felt so bad for her. She was in so much pain that even the nurse on

duty came in to try to comfort her. I really didn't know what else to do. After a while I walked out of the room, and said a prayer for her that God would take her soon. I tried to be upbeat and reminisce with her husband and children about the things Anna did, and made them laugh. Then it was time for me to leave. I hugged her husband and each of her children. I didn't want to cry in front of them, but this was not the way I wanted to see Anna go. I remember having conversations with Anna as she put her affairs in order. All she wanted was for her husband to find another person to love the way he loved her. As for her children, she hoped that they would be happy with their choices, and remember her fondly."

That evening Amie got a call from one of their friends that Anna was gone and that the family was in the process of making funeral arrangements.

"I later found out that Anna died on her husband's birthday. What a hard memory to have. But I know that he loved her very much, and now had to find a way to get along without her. At the funeral her husband, children, grandchildren, and many of Anna's extended family members, as well as close friends, were there. Her life was displayed by lots of photos. Anna loved pictures. She posted all of the current ones on Facebook, and carried small albums of her grandchildren. There was an open casket and one could tell that it was her. If Anna had been there, I don't think that she would have been comfortable with all the love

and attention that was being expressed towards her. She wasn't a 'touchy feely' type of person. She showed love by doing things for others. At the funeral, the priest talked about the person of Anna. He told the audience that she was devoted to her family and friends, and had gotten closer to God. How true that was. She is with Him now, along with my Aaron. I wonder what she thought of him as she met him. Every so often I think of Anna when certain situations arise, and tell her that I wish she was still here with us."

Amie told me that she will always miss her dear friend, who reached out to her in her moment of sadness and helped her move on with her life.

HONOR TO A DIFFERENT GENERATION

Amie shared with me that she never met her grandparents. Alex had two sets of them growing up. Each of their children are named after them.

> "Alex's grandparents came from Russia and Romania back around the turn of the twentieth century and raised their families in the city. Alex's mother had an older sister who died from a blood transfusion while she was suffering from chicken pox. She was only thirteen at the time. His mother had two younger brothers who were twins...now [she was] the oldest child in her family."
>
> Amie told me a story that when his mother was around four years old, her mother sent her to live with an aunt who had no children, because her brothers were sickly and needed more attention than she did. Her mother wanted her back after two years, but it was a difficult transition for her. The aunt really had trouble letting her go. She loved her like she was her own daughter. It took a while for her mother and sister to see

each other without pain. Eventually, they worked things out. Alex's mother doesn't remember experiencing this. She was very close to her brothers, her mother and especially her father.

Alex's father had a younger sister who is still living. He died at the age of ninety-four. He was a quiet man, and one of few words. The best way to describe him was that he always had a smile on his face, and he wasn't bothered by much.

Alex's father's father was married three times, because each of his wives died of some physical ailment. His first wife, who was Alex's father's mother, was a good woman. His father was a furrier who had come from Russia. He cut the skins off the furs, so that they could be sewed into coats. Both sets of parents were very involved in their children's lives."

When Alex's parents finally met each other, Amie told me that they lived a few blocks from one another.

"The story has been told by Alex's mother that they met through a housekeeper that worked for both of their parents. It was during WWII in the early 1940's. The draft was on, and within three months of their meeting they were married. Alex's father said, 'When you find a good thing, why wait?' Indeed!"

Back then, Alex's mother told Amie that she wanted to be different when it came to the wedding dress.

"Instead of a white dress, she got married in a blue one. They had a traditional Jewish wedding, and her father owned a nightclub where the reception took place. She said that it was lovely. Her twin brothers were their best men, and Alex's father's sister was her matron of honor in the wedding party. After the wedding and honeymoon, they settled near their parents' apartment where they would live for nearly ten years. During that time, they had their first child, a beautiful red-headed little girl. As she grew, she wanted her parents to have another baby. Five years later they had Alex."

Two years after Alex was born, his family moved to the suburbs and bought a house. "They saved up all their money for the down payment, and to their surprise, Alex's mother's father gave her the down payment money for the house. What a wonderful gift! This was the house in which Alex and his sister grew up."

Alex's parents' relationship was an interesting one, Amie recalled.

"They took on traditional roles. His father worked in the city and became profoundly deaf because of his work near the entrance/exit to the subway station where he co-owned a luncheonette. The noise of the trains constantly moving caused him to lose his hearing. He met a lot of interesting people. He would leave the house at five-thirty in the morning and come home in time for dinner around six-thirty at night. Alex's mother would have dinner ready when he arrived home. He worked at this business for about twenty-nine years."

Alex commented to Amie that even with that kind of schedule, his father was always willing to spend time with his children. On many occasions, Alex and his father would have a game of catch in the back yard, even though his father was tired from getting up early and working all day.

"When his father retired from being in the luncheonette business, Alex found his father work as a taxi driver at a local taxi cab company in their town. It was only three miles away from their home and he walked to work every morning, and in all kinds of weather. He worked there for thirty years. He was about eighty-six years old when he finally had to retire completely. It was a difficult thing for him to retire, because he loved to drive and enjoyed meeting all kinds of people and talking with them. Everyone liked him and enjoyed his company. He would tell his passengers about all the places he and Alex's mother had traveled to."

They went everywhere; from Israel (fourteen times) to Antarctica, and everywhere in between, Amie shared.

"He brought a hat from most of the places they traveled to. In his quiet way, he was an adventurer. He always said that it was nice to travel, but he liked coming home. It was the best place to live. Toward the end of his life, he needed a pacemaker and a colon operation. He didn't survive the colon operation due to the fact that the stitches weren't healing properly. When his wife was not with him in the hospital, all he could talk

about was wanting more time with her. He had an unconditional love for her. Alex learned that from him. He never complained, and his beautiful blue eyes always sparkled when he looked at her. Alex's mother called their relationship a love affair. She said that they never argued. That was because Alex's father was easy going. Whatever she wanted, she got. It was always her way. He also used to say that he had the best family. They were married for sixty-seven years. Alex's mother was a classy lady. She was always dressed femininely and had make-up on, especially red lipstick. She always re-applied it after dinner like clockwork. Alex's father used to say a lady should always wears a skirt. Alex's mother said that he liked looking at her legs. "

As the grandchildren arrived, they were happy to see their family expanding. Amie told me that Alex's sister had two children before he and Amie had their first. Alex's sister had three children, two boys and a girl. Amie had four children, three boys and a girl.

"As each of our children was growing up, it became a family tradition to have dinner with Alex's parents every Sunday. Every time we went to a restaurant we needed a big table to fit all of us. That was the main time our children got together when they were younger. Now as young adults, they keep in touch with each other through Facebook. When Alex's father passed away that tradition changed. Now it was Alex and his sister's turn to take their mother to dinner with their children.

She felt so lost without Alex's father. It was hard for her to adjust."

Amie asked her if they ever talked about what one would do if the other went first. She said no. Maybe if they did she would have had hope to see him again.

This continued until...his mother needed more care. She was no longer able to stay by herself. Alex and his sister started to take turns to keep her company. During the weekdays, she went to a senior center.

"Alex and I took her to our house on the weekends to give his sister a break. Within two years, Alex's mom was in need of twenty-four hour care. We couldn't take care of her any more. Alex and his sister are good children, and they visit her frequently. I have gone occasionally to see her, but find it very sad that this woman doesn't remember things the way they happened. She and her husband had a very extraordinary life together. What a generation to have come from! They saw all of the newest technologies come forth for society. Very few in their generation went to college. They did. Alex's mother studied to be a concert pianist. His father studied business. She loved classical music, and took Alex's father to concerts and plays. That's how they spent their free time together. They were a real unit."

One of Amie's sons asked Alex's father which era he liked better, now or when he was growing up. He replied, "When I was growing up." They lived an outstanding life, and saw so

much of the world. They always came back with pictures and little gifts. His parents accepted things as life brought it to them. Toward the end of his life, they were always together. They worked as a team as age crept in the way. They called each other partners. They truly were.

GRANDCHILDREN

The cycle of life continued to flow, and Amie and Alex were at the stage of being grandparents themselves. Amie was amazed that she had arrived at this place in life. Their son Samuel and his wife Ann had given them their first grandchild.

> "Everyone has wanted to spend time with her to get to know her, and love on her. She was born over five years ago. She is a beautiful little girl named Grace. The grandparents on both sides have looked at family pictures of Samuel and Ann when pictures were printed by a regular camera. Grace looks like both of her parents at once. She has her mother's eyes, and her father's face. She is so cute, and very girly. She has brought so much love and attention to all the other members of the extended family. Both sets of grandparents love her as if she was their own child. Their hearts just got bigger and made room for more."

Grace is at the stage where she knows everyone in the family by name. She calls Alex "Pop-Pop" and Amie calls "Nana." She is so smart, and wants to know about everything. Her parents are very good parents and work as a team. They now have

another baby. His name is Edmond. He resembles Grace, and has a sweet disposition. Grace is now the big sister. Grace will teach her new brother everything she knows. He will teach her new things, too.

Amie said that she and Alex want Grace and Edmond to be healthy and happy children, learn about God, and learn how much they love them.

"We just want to make sure that we can make lasting memories with them. What a wonderful gift it is to be a grandparent! We are looking forward for all of our children to have children. I have told them that I expect to be a grandmother of eight. That is a great number."

THE GREAT GATSBY

Amie and Alex's daughter Elisabeth had been working on leaving home ever since she started college, Amie told me.

> "When she was in her third year of college, she moved into the dormitory. Elisabeth liked being on her own. She would come and visit, but preferred living by herself. She was independently-minded for most things, even though she was financially dependent."
>
> [Elisabeth] is her mother and father's "daughter girl." After completing a degree in Journalism, she decided to pursue law. This was such an appropriate choice. Law school was very demanding, and Elisabeth had some challenges with her health as well, but she worked through it. She graduated from law school number one in her class. She was the valedictorian on the day of graduation, and we had the joy of hearing her give a speech to all the graduates and dignitaries, one of whom was our state's Chief Judge.

After graduation, she landed a job with a prestigious law firm that she had worked for as an intern the previous summer. She moved near her job, and really enjoys that kind of lifestyle. She

comes to all family gatherings, and even coordinates them. Amie and Alex are so proud of her accomplishments. Amie told me that she tells everyone that she is thrilled about Elisabeth's success.

"When she was in law school, Elisabeth had met the man of her dreams — a guy named Shawn. They dated for four years and began to think about tying the knot. On Christmas Eve, her beau called up Alex in the middle of dinner and asked if he could give them his blessing. Shawn told him that he was planning this within a couple of weeks. It turned out to be that very night! Elisabeth called us around 11:30 that night and told us the news. She even sent us a picture of the ring on our cell phones. It was a very pretty ring. He did well.
Now all of Elisabeth's focus was on planning her wedding. She decided to use a warehouse that could be converted into a wedding venue. Elisabeth asked me to accompany her to the city as she looked for dresses. I asked her if we could go to the famous one that's on television, and she said yes. We went there and the place was beautiful. All of the dresses Elisabeth tried on fit her to a T. Nothing looked bad on her. Even her future mother in-law agreed with me. Finally, she found a really pretty and feminine dress from another boutique.
Elisabeth did not want everything traditional. She wanted to get married under a *chuppah* (marriage canopy) made of flowers. She also wanted Alex to wear a dark blue suit, and she helped me find a pretty black dress that was perfect for the occasion. I helped Elisabeth get some extra jewelry to go with her dress.

During the summer prior to the wedding, I had a bridal shower for her at a quaint tea house. Her best girlfriend hosted. We played games and there was a question and answer video with Shawn. Elisabeth knew nothing about the video and was taken completely by surprise. It was lovely.

Elisabeth had arranged to have our hair and makeup done right before the wedding ceremony. The hairdresser and make-up artist made me look really good. She even put false eyelashes on me. I had never worn them before. Elisabeth wore her grandmother's diamond pendant necklace. It looked stunning on her, especially since Elisabeth looks a lot like her grandmother. Her brothers and their wives looked so handsome and beautiful, of course. Her youngest brother, Seth, looked so grown up. The grandchildren were dressed up, too. They were so cute! Seth helped take care of the grandchildren during the reception with such ease. He likes being an uncle. The wedding went well, and the reception went on past midnight. It was very impressive. Her theme for the wedding was *the Great Gatsby*.

Elisabeth's dress was elegant, and Shawn was dressed in a tuxedo that fit that time period. All of the tables had quotes from that book. Elisabeth had the venue decorated like a magazine picture. Everything was perfect. She and Shawn went on a secret honeymoon that only a few friends and family knew about. I was so happy when they got back safely. They then got an apartment in the borough where Elisabeth was born."

LEAVING THE NEST

It had been a pleasure for Amie and Alex to see Seth, their fourth child, make his plans to leave the nest.

> "He has learned much from all his siblings, since they helped raise him from the very start. They have all had a part in guiding his future. Samuel gave to Seth his interest in sports and finance. Seth's interest in video games, the guitar and graphic design came from Benjamin. Seth's drive for excellence came from Elisabeth, along with her being his personal fashion designer. He has relied on their love and advice, and vice versa. He holds a special place in the family because he helped complete it."

Amie shared with me that Seth had graduated high school, and was in his third year of college studying engineering, electrical engineering, and computer science. He lives on campus when he is in school. "It was a difficult adjustment for me at first, but I got used to it. Soon Seth will be out on his own after he graduates from college."

So now Amie and Alex are back to where they started in this family, just the two of them. Their nest is temporarily empty,

but their hearts are always open for the family birthdays, holidays and just having dinners together. Amie shared with me that she enjoys their interaction. "I have watched them take care of each other. That is what family is all about. Alex and I have lots of love and admiration for the strong adults and good human beings they have become. It's their turn to make their path in life, serving their families and others that come along the way."

THE FORTIETH YEAR

The time has come when Alex and Amie had been married for forty years. Who could have imagined it? Definitely not Amie. The year had been filled with life's busyness, which included building a new house for Amie. Amie shared with me that since all of her children were now out of the house, it was time for her to have a house to meet her physical needs.

"Alex and I looked and looked for a house that had everything on one floor. There were many we went to see, but they were too small for me to maneuver in. One day we saw a model house in our area, and went in to look at it. It was beautiful. The builder happened to be there, and I asked him if he could build a ranch house, since the model was a colonial house. He said that he could. We got all excited. He showed us an architectural floor plan of a house he was building in a town close to us. 'Wow!' I thought. That house was a bit big for me. Yet this was a start. Alex and I kept going back to talk to him to gather information. We eventually got in contact with his architect to draw up a plan for us. I went on the computer and looked up what kind of house I

wanted for over three hours. She took my ideas, and she came back with a beautiful house plan that would be semi-handicapped accessible just in case I ever needed a wheel chair. That was the start of an interesting adventure, since Alex and I never built a house before. It took less than a year to build. There were a lot of decisions to be made about what materials were needed to build it, the costs, and bank approval for construction, including picking out things, such as kitchen cabinets, lighting, flooring, paint colors, window styles, siding on the house and bathroom fixtures, toilets just for starters. Packing and moving had its own story. All I could say about it was that it was back-breaking work. Longtime friends worked over three weeks to get it all together. They deserved a real vacation after all that. It was so much work! Ileana, our lovely daughter in-law, helped us with all of these details, and kept us focused on what needed to be completed. Alex and I don't think that the results would have been as lovely without her vision, and her unending patience with us. I told Benjamin that this house is for the grandchildren to have memories of our family. It has become the new focal point for the family."

Alex wanted to have a party for their fortieth year together.

"It turned out that there were two parties, one for the congregation and one for the family. We also invited our new neighbors to join the celebration. Alex surprised me with a diamond tennis bracelet as a gift. I had always hinted that I would like to

have one someday, but wasn't expecting it with all of the expenses of the house. I found out later that he was planning it a few months back with a friend and her son who worked in the renowned Tiffany's jewelry store. He knew the difference in what was considered quality and what was not. He picked out a beautiful piece of jewelry. Alex is a contented man, with me by his side, as we enter this new stage in life. It doesn't seem that long ago that our lives were put together. I tell people that the only way I really know that it has been this long is by the ages of our children. May we be able to enjoy the rest of our lives together and leave a legacy for our children to follow after us."

REFLECTIONS

As one grows older, it is vitally important to be able to look back at one's life either positively or negatively with a clear pair of glasses on. Nothing is completely black or white. Much of life is filled with various colors in between those opposite book ends. Childhood should be filled with happy memories, yet for Amie it was not. Those painful memories never really go away. They have tried to come back when the stresses of life became overwhelming. The hurtful voices attached to these memories have faded in the distance as life became filled with good things as she was able to focus on them instead of the hurts of the past.

Experiences make us who we are. Yes, Amie might have wished that things were different now that she has seen what could have been possible by raising her own children. Amie has come to realize that she cannot change what happened in the past, but can learn from it, and that her past does not have to define her as a person. That is why the past is the past.

Amie found out that she did not have to make people like her, or always agree with her. She could be herself and be open to those with whom she felt comfortable. She made sure that her children had a better past than she did by being as truthful with them as possible. Amie had the right to be happy. The only

way to be truly happy is to be thankful and never take anything for granted, because there are no guarantees in life.

At times it was hard for Amie to focus on the present, especially when she faced difficult situations, but somehow she got the strength to go through it by loving and understanding people around her that were a gift from God. Amie now believes that there should always be room left in one's heart for hope and faith.

Hope is defined as the feeling of what is wanted that is obtainable in order to change the outcome of life events. If it is not there at the moment, take some time to put it there. Having hope is what brings its partner, which is faith. The Bible defines faith as "the substance of things hoped for, and the evidence of things not seen," (see Hebrews 11:1). It is by faith that you can look to create a better tomorrow. Amie found that God will be there in your corner, urging you on to keep going no matter what (see Jeremiah 29: 11-14). He will bring people into your life to help get it done.

An educator by the name of Eric Erikson said that there are eight stages of development in a person's life. He believed that the point of growing older was to be able to give back to others, without thinking of oneself; it is the ability to leave a legacy behind for the next generation to take up the baton and go forward. By doing this, one is able to judge himself by his accomplishments and failures. In so doing, he can have a sense of integrity about life, instead of feeling despair that something was left out and could not be replaced.

Amie told me that she has thought about this process very deeply. She has worked very hard with each obstacle that crossed her path, striving not to see herself as being unwanted, abandoned or forsaken.

"These kinds of dark and loud emotions are based on lies. Lies make a person feel put down and instill a desire to get back at those who said them with just as much hurt, and interfere with the process of building a productive life. The real revenge in life is one's success over what could have been a tragedy. Some might argue that sometimes it is okay to tell a 'white lie.' It can be protection from pain. That is true, but only for a while. The truth eventually comes out, and with it brings out more pain in the end. Lies are selfish in nature, and lead to wrong conclusions. Lies do not have power to overcome what is true. Knowing the truth brings acceptance and the feeling of accomplishment to keep going."

Amie also had to sort out what to believe in. She had a great helper in her belief when the Lord took her up in His arms and made a path for her despite those very difficult beginnings. This was true even though at times there were parts of her that responded to life situations as if she were still that "much afraid little one." This was because many situations brought back those old memories of what caused the pain, shame and isolation which had affected her so deeply.

All people need to be wanted and loved. Isn't that what life is about — to be loved and to love in return? Love demonstrates that one has value, and is worth something to someone. That is why it is so easy to love a child. They love unconditionally, when there is real love within a family. It is the love of the family that gives a child support and reassurance that life will go on.

In working on this book with Amie, I have seen her work hard at explaining what went on in her life as well as what was in her heart. Even though Amie never really had a family of her

own and felt that she missed out on one somehow, someway, various people were brought into her life to teach her the true meaning of family. As she was able to learn and grasp what she saw, it gave her the courage and determination to create one of her own. Many of these people became her closest friends. By showing her such kindness and consideration, they helped her dream about having a future, her own voice, and to have confidence in herself.

Amie broke the probable pattern of single motherhood, and a possible abuse cycle, by getting married to a kind and loving man. This helped her take the higher ground. She learned that this involved the principle of doing unto others as you would want others to do to you (see Matthew 7:12).

Alex couldn't take care of all of Amie's hurts, but he was able to give her his strength to move forward. He took on the role of being that special someone in her corner. She had to find out what she was willing to live by in order to provide a stable home. This came from working with a therapist, Luisa, as well as a few close friends who proved their loyalty and trust in her. She wasn't that defenseless little girl any more. She needed help coming to terms with what she was given and found a way to accept it. Amie wanted me to share with those who read this book that the serenity prayer demonstrates how this can be done. It states: "God grant me the serenity to accept the things I cannot change, the courage to change the things I can, and the wisdom to know the difference."

Her husband brought into her life the idea of what it means to be thankful. It is not having what one wants that counts. Rather, it is wanting what one has that counts (Helen Keller). Being able to love and be loved helped Amie to be thankful, as well as be emotionally connected to others. Anything good comes with a price, and should not be taken for granted or thrown away.

Amie learned that other people's opinions were fine, but she did not necessarily have to agree with them. It was all right to agree to disagree. The mark of a true friendship is having the ability to spend time with someone who does not agree on all subjects, but nevertheless values your opinion. Amie also learned that no one is happy all the time, but there can be a sense of contentment in the midst of trying circumstances. There is always someone else who might have it worse.

So what does all this mean? Amie says:

> "It means that life is what you make of it. We can't always control what happens, but one thing we can do is make the best of it. You can make it, even if you don't think you can. As long as one has life, there is hope. The process of growth, positively or negatively, is inevitable and comes with change, whether we like it or not. Nothing stays the same. We are never alone. The Lord himself said that He would never leave us or forsake us even until the end of the age (see Mathew 28: 20 and Hebrews 13:5). He will always provide someone to help us along the way. The key is to be able to find healing from the wounds of being and feeling unwanted, abandoned and forsaken. It takes a lifetime to heal as wounds get scraped off and recovered. Yet through much love and forgiveness, life gets better and more rewarding as one is able to reach out to others. I have found that no one goes through life without some kind of pain. We are all flawed human beings that have a light inside of us if we are willing to let it out to shine on others."

Amie has come a long way from the time when she did not know what kind of life she would be able to have. She told me that being alone does not have the same effect on her like it did when she was younger. She has acquired skills to keep herself company and has learned how to mother herself, as Luisa taught her, when she is upset about something. "There will always be a part of me that will miss what I didn't have, but at this point it is a very, very small part."

Amie no longer needs to fear getting in trouble, nor does she need to prove herself to anyone. Neither does she have anything to be ashamed of anymore. Her family loves her and she loves them, and that is all that matters. Alex's parents once told her that if one has family and a few good friends that one could count on his hand, he is truly blessed. All she longed for has come to pass through hard work, and along the way she was given many gifts.

> "Jane asked me once during one of our conversations if the feeling of being alone would ever go away. I shared with her that I felt that it changed as one was more able to be comfortable with the changes life brings. The truth is that we really are all alone. We are born alone, and we will die alone. It is part of life. Yet, in between those times we don't have to be lonely. There will always be someone there, even if we can't always see who it is."

Growing up without a real mother made it more difficult for Amie to understand how life worked. Many things did not come naturally to her, as it did to others who were in her life. She told me that she almost never takes anything for granted. She found out that she made lots of mistakes, even though she

tried not to, and wondered if she would ever get to the other side. Sometimes it seemed to her that she had to discuss things "tooth and nail," or as Alex would say, "beat a dead horse," in order to come to a mutual understanding on something.

Even so, she never stopped fighting for her children. Her focus for her children was on always their safety, and the ability for them to take care of themselves when they were old enough to be on their own. Amie told me that she wanted to thank them for what they taught her. They made her very proud. They gave her confidence that she could care for them in spite of all of her fears and her concerns for them, as well as, for how others would see her.

To balance her tendency to be over-protective, Alex was able to take a step back and approach a situation with the attitude that the concerns for the children should be for their sakes, not for his own feelings. Alex was more interested in what was good for them as opposed to what he wanted at the moment. He had the ability not to take things personally in order to do the right thing.

When Amie looks back at her children's accomplishments, she is in awe.

> "My heart for them was to provide an environment so that they could be free to express themselves and find out who they were and what they wanted to be. They experienced different kinds of struggles than I did. Yet for the most part, one could say they could be considered normal growing pains."

She hopes that they can look back and say that they felt loved and cared for despite her shortcomings of being head strong and very opinionated, though never wanting to cause any harm.

Amie had to be willing to forgive. She needed to let go of the hurtful feelings and the emotional power attached to those memories that caused her pain. It did not mean that she forgot what happened, but that she would release the person or persons who were responsible for that pain. It becomes a decision, not a feeling (see Luke 23:34).

One of the meanings of forgiveness in the dictionary is the willingness to be forgiven. It works both ways. They are really tied together. How interesting. One's ability to forgive is also related to one's ability to be forgiven. "That is where God's grace comes in, because He is the only one who gives us the strength to do it in the first place. From a human point of view, the ability to forgive is a real growth process."

Included in the ability to forgive is the ability to put feelings of anger and frustration over what happened in their proper place.

> "Many people in similar situations either are angry all the time or stuff it down inside of them and don't know how to let it out in a constructive manner. Negative anger interferes with making proper choices, having self- control, and being able to deal with difficulties that inevitably come along the way. It demonstrates that someone else is in control. On the other hand, positive anger becomes a tool for change."

Freud said that the value of having a good life is to find value in the ability to work. Learning how to keep a job was the tool that helped Amie learn the value of work. She realized that she could help someone else and that her guidance was beneficial, and it strengthened her confidence.

"Even though working at a job is working for someone else, in reality you are really working for yourself. Every new skill that is learned helps you for the next one. If you are willing to help others, it gives the work that you do more value, and makes working more enjoyable. The ability to give something to someone and not expect something in return is a sign of maturity. Concentrate on what you can do and not on what you can't do. This way the focus is not always inward toward self, and keeps things in the positive (see Colossians 3:23). It is not useful to compare yourself to someone else. It will take away your strength to keep focused."

The dictionary defines hope as the feeling that what is wanted can be had, something to look forward to, as well as something to believe, desire or trust (see Hebrews 11:1). Having hope creates an atmosphere to look towards the future. Never let it go.

Amie said that life is gift with other people in it to make you what one is supposed to be. "No one has the capacity to control everything that happens. There is always a way to make it even if one thinks there isn't. The Lord will provide someone to walk alongside to help when life becomes overwhelming and too much to handle."

Is Amie that "Much Afraid Little One" anymore? The answer truthfully is no and, occasionally, yes. The voices of fear have always been in the back of her mind, and occasionally when they rise up, they do not stay in her mind as long as they have in the past. Amie now has found more tools and information to deal with them. Knowledge is power (see Hosea 4:6). "It is human to fear things that are unknown and question those things we do not understand. That is why having faith is so

important. Faith is a positive force to forge ahead. Fear makes one retreat and look for a safer place."

Amie shared with me that her second son, Benjamin, saw his mother as someone who tried really hard to muster up a wall of protection against the world. He believed that this wall of protection was all her fears. He described it as if his mother was the child holding on to a teddy bear for dear life so that no one would take it away from her. He also wanted Amie to know that if she would allow her faith to grow, she would understand that it was not the teddy bear that was the real issue. God's heart for her has always been there by her side. He was the one who wrapped his arms around her to protect her so that others would not take away what was precious to her and not the other way around. She did not have to work so hard to hold on to things because God has taken care of her by giving her a real family. Therefore, if Amie should experience fear in the future, she would need to remember that God's perfect love casts out fear (see 1 John 4:18). "What an insight from a young man who exhibits unconditional love to those he loves!"

Amie has told me many times that we all make mistakes. "No one is perfect, and we shouldn't expect people in our lives to be perfect. It is unrealistic. Being afraid only takes away the energy that is needed to be truly invested emotionally in a positive way in other people's lives."

Amie has come to believe that there is always a chance for good, even in the bad.

> "As much as possible, live in the truth of the present, not in the past. Be prepared to work hard, cry hard, accept your faults, and use them as tools to make better life choices for yourself and others who are in your life. Reach out to those who can be trusted to help navigate

trouble spots. Never give in or give up. There is always hope. Sometimes there will be a need to have time to rest and re-group, but one still has to get up and keep moving forward. No one gets out of this life without struggles. Struggle is a part of life, and overcoming its obstacles is the winning prize. Most importantly, remember God gives us chances to fix what can be fixed and the strength to do it. It doesn't matter how long it takes to fix things. Leave alone what can't be fixed, and ask for grace to accept it. His mercies are new every morning (see Lamentations 3:22-23). It is knowing that there is always going to be a tomorrow as long as there a sunrise and sunset in the earth."

In conclusion, Amie wanted to share a song written by a Christian song-writer named Bill Gaither that describes in a nutshell what she feels really happened to her. The following are the words to this song:

(verse)
If there ever were dreams
That were lofty and noble
Those were my dreams at the start
And my hope for life's best were the hopes
That I harbor down deep in my heart
But my dreams turned to ashes
And my castles all crumbled, my fortune turned to loss
So I wrapped it all in the rags of life
And laid it at the cross.

(chorus)

Something beautiful, something good,
All my confusion, He understood.
All I had to offer Him was brokenness and strife.
But He made something beautiful of my life.

(Copyright © 1972, Lyrics by Gloria Gaither/Music by Bill Gaither)

So, then what can be said of this "Much Afraid Little One" whose name was Amie? She made it despite being afraid for most of her life. Perfect love casts out fear. Fear has torment and contributes to an unsound mind (see 2 Timothy 1:7). Through it all, these are common experiences of life we all share because we are human (see 1 Corinthians 10:13).

Amie has come through it with a wonderful guiding force behind her, in front of her and all around her so that her crooked way was made straight (see Luke 3:5 and Isaiah 42:16).

Amie would like to invite the reader to explore the idea that when one looks to God for help, he is always there to give it, and to be that guiding light and strength if we let Him (see Proverbs: 3:5-6).

In Hebrews 4:14-16 it states:

> "Seeing then that we have a great High Priest who has passed through the heavens, Jesus the Son of God, let us hold fast our confession. For we do not have a High Priest who cannot sympathize with our weakness, but was in all points tempted as we are, yet without sin. Let us therefore come boldly to the throne of grace that we may obtain mercy and find grace to help in the time of need."

In the book of Mathew 11: 28-30 it states:

> "Come unto me all ye that labor and are heavy laden, and I will give you rest. Take my yoke upon you and learn of me, for I am gentle and lowly in heart, and you will find rest for your souls. For My yoke is easy, and my burden is light."

Amie says, "This is the power that helps one use their voice and gives one the grace to overcome life's many obstacles. No one can make it in life alone. We weren't designed that way, nor should we have to."

> "Amie, like me, is no longer unwanted, abandoned, nor forsaken. You see, Amie is me, and I am she. My life has been a journey of finding out who I really am, becoming a woman who I never thought I could be. A successful wife, mother, grandmother, a true friend, a person who has learned to accept herself, and who found faith in God. He who has loved me faithfully and unconditionally. I have discovered that I truly have never been left alone."

The words from the song entitled "You'll Never Walk Alone," from the musical *Carousel* express that thought perfectly.

When you walk through a storm, hold your head up high,
And don't be afraid of the dark,
At the end of the storm is a golden sky,
And the sweet silver song of a lark.
Walk on through the wind, Walk on through the rain,
Though your dreams be tossed and blown, Walk on, Walk on

With hope in your heart, and you'll never walk alone,
You'll never walk alone, you'll never walk alone.

(Rodgers and Hammerstein Song Book Copyright 1958, 1968 by Williamson Music, Inc. Simon and Schuster and Williamson Music, Inc. New York)

"Music says it best. It describes what is really important in life. Never close your heart to others, and keep those whom you love even closer, because they have the true ingredient that has the power to make one whole."